Argumentat
Understanding and Shaping Arguments

Instructor's Manual

Argumentation

Understanding and Shaping Arguments

fifth edition

Instructor's Manual

James A. Herrick
Hope College

Strata Publishing, Inc.
State College, Pennsylvania

Instructor's Manual
Argumentation: Understanding and Shaping Arguments

9 8 7 6 5 4 3 2 1

Copyright © 2005, 2007, 2011, 2015 by James A. Herrick
All rights reserved. Printed in the United States of America. No part of this publication may be reproduced, stored in a retrieval system, or transmitted in any form or by any means whatsoever (including electronic, mechanical, photocopying, scanning, or otherwise), without the prior written permission of the publisher.

Published by:
Strata Publishing, Inc.
P.O. 1303
State College, PA 16804

telephone: 814-234-8545
web site: www.stratapub.com

Cover photo: A red marble inside a drawn circle ©iStock.com/John_Brueske

ISBN-13: 978-1-891136-35-1

Contents

Sample Syllabus vii

PART I: Goals, Skills, and Functions of Argumentation 1

Chapter 1: An Introduction to Argumentation 3
Chapter 2: The Elements of Arguments 7
Chapter 3: Tools for Analyzing Arguments 13

PART II: The Conditions of Constructive Argumentation 27

Chapter 4: Ethical Advocacy 29
Chapter 5: Reasonable Arguments, Reasonable People 33

PART III: Support: The Content of Arguments 39

Chapter 6: Evaluating Evidence 41
Chapter 7: Locating and Evaluating Sources of Evidence 45
Chapter 8: Using Statistics as Evidence 49
Chapter 9: Using Testimony as Evidence 57

PART IV: Validity: The Structure of Arguments 63

Chapter 10: Validity in Conditional and Enumeration Arguments 65
Chapter 11: Validity in Categorical Arguments 75

PART V: Linguistic Consistency: Language in Argument 85

Chapter 12: Definition in Argument 87
Chapter 13: Ambiguity, Equivocation, and Other Language Considerations 93

PART VI: Types and Tests of Arguments 103

Chapter 14: Analogies, Examples, Metonymy, and Narratives 105
Chapter 15: Reasoning about Causes 119
Chapter 16: Moral and Practical Arguments 133
Chapter 17: Essential Nature Arguments 141
Chapter 18: Fallacies and Appeals 149

APPENDICES: Developing and Adapting Your Case 157

Appendix A: Policy Case Construction: The Structure of Debate 159
Appendix B: Adapting Arguments to an Audience 163

Exams and Written Assignments 169

Exam I: Chapters 1–10 171
Exam II: Chapters 11–18, Appendices A and B 177
Written Assignments 183

Sample Syllabus

This course seeks to develop those skills of argumentation involved in effective reasoning and communication. In developing these skills, we will study various types of arguments, note the tests to which each is susceptible, and analyze examples of arguments. Other topics covered in the course include the ethics of advocacy, the types and tests of evidence, preparing a case, and adapting it to an audience.

The **goals** of this class are:

1: To introduce you to the basic theory of argument.

2: To improve your skills as a critical consumer of arguments.

3: To enhance your ability to present sound arguments.

The **text** for this course is James A. Herrick, *Argumentation: Understanding and Shaping Arguments,* 5th ed. (State College, Pa.: Strata, 2015).

The assignments and exams for the course include:

Argument analysis project (20%)

Presentation (10%)

Homework assignments (10%)

Final (20%)

Quizzes (total of 10%)

Midterms (2 at 10% each—20%)

Participation, including exercises and attendance (10%).

PLAN OF STUDY

Week 1

Day	Topic	Assignment
Monday	Overview	
Wednesday	Part I: Goals, Skills, and Functions of Argumentation Chapter 1: Introduction to Argumentation	Exercises A and B.
Friday	Chapter 1	Exercise C.

Week 2

Day	Topic	Assignment
Monday	Chapter 2: The Elements of Argument	Exercises A, B, and C.
Wednesday	Chapter 2	Exercise D.
Friday	Chapter 3: Tools for Analyzing Arguments	Exercises A and B.

Week 3

Day	Topic	Assignment
Monday	Chapter 3	Exercises C and D.
Wednesday	Part II: The Conditions of Constructive Argumentation Chapter 4: Ethical Advocacy	Exercise A presented in class.
Friday	Chapter 4	Exercises B and C.

Week 4

Day	Topic	Assignment
Monday	Chapter 5: Reasonable Arguments, Reasonable People	Exercise A or D presented in class.
Wednesday	Chapter 5	Exercises B and C.
Friday	Part III: Support: The Content of Arguments Chapter 6: Evaluating Evidence	Exercises A and B.

Week 5

Day	Topic	Assignment
Monday	Chapter 7: Locating and Evaluating Sources of Evidence	Exercise A, B, or C presented in class. Exercise D.
Wednesday	Chapter 8: Using Statistics as Evidence	Exercises A and B.
Friday	Chapter 9: Using Testimony as Evidence	Exercise A.

Week 6

Day	Topic	Assignment
Monday	Part IV: Validity: The Structure of Arguments Chapter 10: Validity in Conditional and Enumeration Arguments	Exercise A.
Wednesday	Chapter 10	Exercises B, C, and D. Review for First Exam: Chapters 1–10.
Friday		First Exam.

Week 7

Day	Topic	Assignment
Monday	Chapter 11: Validity in Categorical Arguments	Exercise A.
Wednesday	Chapter 11	Exercise B.
Friday	Chapter 11	Review.

Week 8

Day	Topic	Assignment
Monday	Part V: Linguistic Consistency: Language in Argument Chapter 12: Definition in Argument	Exercises A, B, and C.
Wednesday	Chapter 13: Ambiguity, Equivocation, and Other Language Considerations	Exercises A and B.
Friday	Chapter 13	Exercises C, D, and E.

Week 9

Day	Topic	Assignment
Monday	Part VI: Types and Tests of Arguments Chapter 14: Analogies, Examples, and Narratives	Exercise A.
Wednesday	Chapter 14	Exercises B and C.
Friday	Chapter 14	Exercises D and E. Exercise F to turn in.

Week 10

Day	Topic	Assignment
Monday	Chapter 15: Reasoning about Causes	Exercises A and B.
Wednesday	Chapter 15: Reasoning about Causes	Exercises C and D. Argument Analysis Assignment discussed in class.
Friday	Chapter 16: Moral and Practical Arguments	Exercises A and B.

Week 11

Day	Topic	Assignment
Monday	Chapter 17: Essential Nature Arguments	Exercise A.
Wednesday	Chapter 18: Fallacies and Appeals	Exercise A.
Friday	Appendices: Developing and Adapting Your Case Appendix A: Policy Case Construction	Exercise A or B (from Instructor's Manual).

Week 12

Day	Topic	Assignment
Monday	Appendix B: Adapting Arguments to an Audience	Exercise A (from Instructor's Manual).
Wednesday		Review for second exam: Chapters 11–18, Appendices A and B.
Friday		Second exam.

Week 13

Day	Topic	Assignment
Monday	Final consultations on projects.	
Wednesday	Presentation schedule and procedure discussed in class.	
Friday		Analysis Projects due.

Week 14

Day	Topic	Assignment
Monday	Projects presented in class.	
Wednesday	Projects presented in class.	
Friday	Projects presented in class.	

Week 15

Day	Topic	Assignment
Monday	Projects presented in class.	
Wednesday	Projects presented in class.	
Friday	Projects presented in class.	

PART I
Goals, Skills, and Functions of Argumentation

Chapter 1
An Introduction to Argumentation

EXERCISES

A. Provide a brief definition for each of the following terms.

advocacy: **The activity of promoting or opposing an idea in public settings.**

argument: **A claim advanced with a reason or reasons in its support.**

argumentation: **The cooperative activity of developing and advancing arguments and of responding to the arguments of others.**

audience: **People for whom we develop our arguments.**

pluralistic culture: **A society composed of groups who see the world from different perspectives, value different activities, hold disparate religious beliefs, and aspire to different goals.**

power: **The capacity to wield influence, to shape important decisions that affect the lives of others.**

procedures: **The rules or guidelines according to which argumentation will take place.**

public discourse: **Open discussion of those issues that potentially affect everyone.**

rule of reason: **The agreement to engage in the cooperative process of argumentation rather than to resolve disagreement by other means.**

values: **Deeply held moral convictions acquired from family, cultural background, religious training, and personal experience.**

B. Identify four of your own values that might influence how you interpret information you hear or read. How did you acquire those values? Identify and describe a situation in which one or more of these values informed an argument you advanced.

C. Suggest one conclusion that you might draw from each of the following facts. Identify the value that led you from the fact to your conclusion.

[This exercise is intended to help students see that different people may draw different conclusions from the same facts.]

1. The National Cancer Institute estimates that four hundred thousand Americans die every year from tobacco-related illnesses.

2. More than two thousand new religions emerged in the United States during the twentieth century.

3. There are one million deaths each year in the US due to medical error on the part of doctors, nurses, pharmacists, and hospital staff.

4. Fifty-five percent of all deaths from gunshots each year in the US are suicides.

5. Cases of adult onset or type 2 diabetes rose from 2 percent of the population in 1973, or 4.2 million Americans, to 7 percent, or 21 million Americans, in 2010.

6. China has the fastest growing economy in the world.

7. The United States imports 58 percent of its petroleum, at a cost of more than $150 billion annually.

8. The United States incarcerates more than 2.3 million people—1 in every 150 of its adult citizens, the highest percentage of any country in the world.

9. More than a million US military personnel who are parents of children still living at home have been deployed in combat arenas over the past decade.

10. Between 2008 and 2013, tuition rates rose by 25 percent at state universities and colleges, and 13 percent at private institutions of higher education.

TEST ITEMS

True or False

1. **T** F Argumentation involves a commitment to sharing our reasons with others as we seek to resolve disagreements.

2. T **F** Argumentation is the effort to persuade others to our point of view, so it does not involve any agreements at the outset.

3. **T** F Through public argumentation facts come to light, and what were previously taken to be facts may be shown false.

4. T **F** Our beliefs, values, and assumptions play a relatively minor role in how we interpret the world we encounter each day.

5. **T** F Our success in addressing "differentness," and in arriving at working agreements out of difference and potential disagreement, will determine the future course of our society.

6. **T** F The rule of reason is the agreement to engage in the cooperative process of argumentation rather than to resolve disagreements by other means.

7. **T** F Whether it is small or large, the audience will usually have a significant impact on how we go about making an argument.

8. **T** F Advocacy and argument are inseparable ideas, for advocacy depends on the presentation of arguments.

9. T **F** Because argumentation is central to the functioning of a democracy, power does not enter the equation when we consider how decisions are made in a free society.

10. **T** F The text attributes various functions to arguments, including to justify, to persuade, and to discover.

11. **T** F The text states that the Internet is perhaps the greatest enhancement to public discourse ever developed.

12. T **F** Fewer people make public arguments because the Internet is such a limited forum.

Terminology

A. Provide the term for each of the following definitions.

1. The activity of promoting or opposing an idea in public settings. **advocacy**

2. A claim advanced with a reason or reasons in its support. **argument**

3. The cooperative activity of developing and advancing arguments and of responding to the arguments of others. **argumentation**

4. A society composed of groups who see the world from different perspectives, value different activities, hold disparate religious beliefs, and aspire to different goals. **pluralistic culture**

5. The capacity to wield influence, to shape important decisions that affect the lives of others. **power**

6. Open discussion of those issues that potentially affect everyone. **public discourse**

7. The agreement to engage in the cooperative process of argumentation rather than to resolve disagreement by other means. **rule of reason**

8. Deeply held moral commitments acquired from family, cultural background, religious training, and personal experience. **values**

9. The rules or guidelines according to which argumentation will take place. **procedures**

10. People for whom we develop our arguments. **audience**

B. Provide definitions for the following terms.

advocacy: **The activity of promoting or opposing an idea in public settings.**

argumentation: **The cooperative activity of developing and advancing arguments and of responding to the arguments of others.**

argument: **A claim advanced with a reason or reasons in its support.**

rule of reason: **The agreement to engage in the cooperative process of argumentation rather than to resolve disagreement by other means.**

power: **The capacity to wield influence, to shape important decisions that affect the lives of others.**

public discourse: **Open discussion of those issues that potentially affect everyone.**

Short Answer

1. What three functions does the text assign to argumentation?
   justify, persuade, discover

2. Provide three potential sources of agreement that may accompany argumentation.
   to resolve disagreement through argumentation, procedures, goals, evidence

3. Identify three ways that values may be involved in argumentation.

   1. Providing a link between a fact and a conclusion drawn from that fact.

   2. Providing a frame for interpreting evidence and assessing options.

   3. Helping diverse groups work through differences and find satisfying compromises.

4. In addition to traditional forms such as conversation, public speaking, nonfiction prose, and talk shows, identify two other forms that the text identifies as means of expressing arguments.

   songs, novels, movies, photographs, visual media

5. The most basic agreement involved in reasoning with another person is the agreement to engage in the cooperative process of argumentation rather than to resolve disagreement by other means. What is this basic agreement called?

   the rule of reason

6. What effect has the Internet had on participation in public discourse?

   More people participate in public discourse now than ever before.

Chapter 2
The Elements of Arguments

EXERCISES

A. Provide a brief definition for each of the following terms.

reason: **A statement advanced for the purpose of establishing a claim.**

conclusion: **A claim that has been reached by a process of reasoning.**

case: **A series of arguments, all advanced to support the same general contention or set of conclusions.**

inference: **A conclusion drawn on the basis of reasons.**

logical sense: **One's sense of how arguments develop.**

indicators: **Words and phrases such as "because" and "therefore" that provide important clues about the reasons and conclusions in an argument.**

cues: **Words or phrases that signal something, other than a reason or a conclusion, about the content of an argument.**

reservation: **A statement in an argument that acknowledges the existence of an argument, evidence, or an attitude opposing the conclusion being advanced.**

B. In each of the following arguments, underline indicators and cues. Draw wavy lines under the conclusions.

<u>Legalizing drugs would radically reduce crime</u> <u>because</u> it would eliminate the high cost of these substances. **[This item was completed in the text as an example.]**

1. One method of acquiring the stem cells necessary for human embryonic stem cell research necessitates destroying human embryos. <u>Therefore</u>, <u>human embryonic stem cell research based on this method is immoral</u>.

2. You must have a dream to act, <u>and</u> you must act to live. <u>Thus</u>, <u>you must have a dream to live</u>.

3. <u>The only way to deal with habitual criminals is incarceration</u>. <u>This is because</u> there are only two possibilities: incarceration or rehabilitation. <u>Though</u> incarceration is an expensive and difficult choice, rehabilitation simply does not work.

4. "Wherever there are laws, there will be lawyers, <u>and</u> where there are lawyers, there will be arguments, <u>for</u> it is by argument that they earn their livings. <u>Thus</u>, <u>where there are laws there will be arguments</u>." [Michael Billig, *Arguing and Thinking: A Rhetorical Approach to Social Psychology*, 2nd ed. (Cambridge, UK: Cambridge University Press, 1996), 28.)]

5. Fines and suspensions are often handed out when athletes turn violent during a game, <u>but</u> widely publicized brawls involving players as well as fans <u>provide clear evidence that</u> tougher measures are needed. [<u>So,</u>] athletes who assault other athletes or fans during a game must be prosecuted under existing criminal statues.

C. Identify each of the following claims as a proposition of fact (**F**), value (**V**), or policy (**P**). [**Terms in *italics* are clues to the type of statement each sentence represents.**]

1. **F:** James Watson and Francis Crick discovered the complex double-helix structure of the DNA molecule in 1959.
2. **V:** Pictures being beamed back from the Hubble Telescope reveal the universe to be a place of *exquisite beauty*.
3. **P:** The United States *should* immediately pass stiffer regulations regulating the use of animals in product research.
4. **F:** The Mercedes Benz SLR *is the fastest* production car on the market from 0 to 60 miles per hour.
5. **P:** Same-sex marriages *should be* made legal in all fifty states.
6. **F:** At the current rate of consumption, Earth's reserves of crude oil *will be* depleted by 2080.
7. **V:** Moving forward with natural gas extraction using fracking is *more important than* developing solar energy technologies.
8. **F:** There *has been a 28 percent increase* in arrests of women for drunk-driving infractions since 1990.
9. **P:** We *must* pass stiffer handgun legislation immediately.
10. **F:** Tabloid headline: "Baby Born Singing Elvis Tunes."

D. <u>Underline</u> any indicators or cues in each of the following examples. Draw a wavy line under the conclusion. Then, label the conclusion as a proposition of fact, value, or policy. (**F, V, P**).

1. **P:** A recent poll by the Pew Research Center revealed that 48 percent of US voters view the Republican Party as friendly to religion, while only 28 percent view the Democratic Party the same way. <u>Thus,</u> Democrats should start now to develop a strategy for winning over the deeply religious voter.
2. **F:** The number of prisoners serving life sentences has now risen to a record 140,610, compared with 34,000 in 1984. This dramatic increase <u>proves that</u> new, stiffer sentencing guidelines are working to keep criminals off the street.
3. **F:** Nuclear arms have prevented war in the past, <u>so</u> they will do the same in the future.
4. **V:** State lotteries are morally unacceptable <u>because</u> they tend to cheat the poorest members of society out of their much-needed monetary resources.

5. **F:** A recent examination of databases from more than 125 US colleges and universities receiving government funds for programs designed to reduce the number of rapes on campus revealed that fewer than one in five men responsible for a sexual assault were expelled.

6. **V:** Decisions in Japanese companies are made by groups, rather than individuals. Thus, decisions in Japanese corporations are made more fairly than in US corporations.

7. **P:** Gambling is an activity that cannot be stopped. Therefore, gambling should be legalized.

8. **V:** The United States's failure to intervene in Rwanda during the 1993 genocide was unconscionable, as this failure revealed an utter disregard for human rights.

9. **F:** US citizens have gained twenty-eight years in life expectancy in the past century. This finding proves that the current system of medical care is working to preserve and improve health.

10. **P:** Instituting a military draft should take place immediately because this is the only equitable way to staff our armed forces.

TEST ITEMS

True or False

1. <u>T</u> F   As defined in the text, an argument will always involve at least one inference.
2. T <u>F</u>   When we identify reasons and conclusions in an argument, all we have to go on is logical sense.
3. <u>T</u> F   The word "because," when used in an argument, signals that a reason will follow.
4. <u>T</u> F   A statement's location in an argument is usually *not* a reliable clue as to whether the statement serves as a reason or a conclusion.
5. T <u>F</u>   The context of controversy is always a sign that an argument is being advanced.
6. <u>T</u> F   The phrase "in addition" is more likely to be a cue than an indicator.
7. <u>T</u> F   Argumentation often involves agreements as well as disagreements.
8. T <u>F</u>   A reservation is introduced by cues such as "therefore" and "so."
9. T <u>F</u>   "The US space program should be abandoned" is a proposition of value.
10. T <u>F</u>   Propositions of fact urge that an action be taken or abandoned.
11. <u>T</u> F   An argument supporting a proposition of value should clarify the criteria that provide the basis for the evaluative judgment.
12. <u>T</u> F   Almost all public controversies involve a mix of agreements and disagreements, as do controversies on a more personal level.
13. T <u>F</u>   In calling a statement "factual," we are saying that the statement is true.
14. <u>T</u> F   A series of assertions, all expressing the same view, does not by itself count as an argument.
15. <u>T</u> F   It is common for propositions of fact and value to be advanced as part of the effort to support a proposition of policy.

Multiple Choice

1. A statement advanced to establish a conclusion.
    a. reservation
    <u>b.</u> reason
    c. indicator
    d. cue
    e. argument

2. A word or phrase that signals a reason or a conclusion will follow.
    a. conclusion
    b. reason
    <u>c.</u> indicator
    d. cue
    e. argument

3. A statement that acknowledges the existence of an argument, evidence, or an attitude opposing the conclusion being advanced.
    a. inference
    <u>b.</u> reservation
    c. conclusion
    d. qualifier
    e. none of the above

4. A reason rooted in observation.
    a. connective
    b. proposition of policy
    c. intermediate conclusion
    d. qualifier
    <u>e.</u> evidence

5. "Lee Harvey Oswald acted alone in killing President Kennedy" is a
    a. proposition of action
    b. proposition of policy
    c. proposition of value
    <u>d.</u> proposition of fact
    e. proposition of judgment

6. A statement that urges an action be taken or discontinued.
    <u>a.</u> proposition of policy
    b. proposition of fact
    c. proposition of value
    d. proposition of action
    e. connective

7. Beliefs, values, assumptions, or generalizations that link some piece of evidence to a conclusion.
    a. propositions of fact
    b. propositions of policy
    c. propositions of value
    d. propositions of action
    <u>e.</u> connectives

8. Statements that report, describe, predict, or make causal claims.
    <u>a.</u> propositions of fact
    b. propositions of policy
    c. propositions of value
    d. propositions of action
    e. connectives

Terminology

Provide the correct term for the following definitions.

1. Statements that report, describe, predict, or make causal claims. **propositions of fact**

2. Statements that advance judgments about morality, beauty, merit, or wisdom. **propositions of value**

3. Statements that urge that an action be taken or discontinued. **propositions of policy**

4. A conclusion drawn on the basis of reasons. **inference**

5. Words or phrases that provide important clues about an argument's reasons and conclusions. **indicators**

6. A statement acknowledging the existence of an argument, evidence, or an attitude opposing the conclusion being advanced. **reservation**

7. Your sense of how arguments develop. **logical sense**

8. Reasons that consist of beliefs, values, assumptions, or generalizations that link a piece of evidence to a conclusion. **connectives**

9. A reason rooted in observation. **evidence**

Short Answer

1. Identify three criteria that a case supporting a proposition of fact should satisfy.
    1. **Advance sufficient evidence to support the factual claim.**
    2. **Clarify and interpret the evidence for the audience.**
    3. **Ensure that the evidence's relevance to the claim is made clear.**

2. Identify two goals of an argument defending a proposition of value.
    1. **clarifying the criteria on the basis of which the value judgment is made**
    2. **providing evidence connecting these criteria to the object being evaluated**

3. What two goals should a case supporting a proposition of fact accomplish?

   1. advance evidence supporting the claim

   2. clarify and interpret the evidence so as to make clear that it supports the factual claim

4. Distinguish between the meanings of the following terms: indicator / cue

   An indicator signals a reason or a conclusion; a cue signals something else about an argument's structure.

5. Distinguish between the meanings of the following terms: evidence / connective

   Both are reasons. However, the connective (a belief, value, or generalization) is a reason that links evidence (some form of observation) to a conclusion.

Chapter 3
Tools for Analyzing Arguments

EXERCISES

A. Scan the following arguments. Draw a wavy line under the conclusion of each example.

   1. **A:** The Federal Reserve Board controls all monetary policy, and thus **B:** functions as a fourth branch of government.

   2. **A:** *Motor News* magazine has named the new Genesis its car of the year, so **B:** you should carefully consider this outstanding luxury sedan.

   3. Because **A:** it would save insurance companies a great deal of money in the long run, and thus **B:** bring down rates for everyone, **C:** genetic testing should be required of everyone applying for life insurance policies.

   4. **A:** Americans used to think only of investing in US companies. **B:** Today, however, a global perspective is vital in your investing, because **C:** today's economy is a global economy.

   5. Because drones will soon be used for everything from product delivery to crowd surveillance, the FAA must move quickly to enact legislation governing drone use.

B. Scan, standardize, and diagram the following arguments. Which argument is deductive? Which is inductive? Your diagrams should also show either independent or complementary reasons.

   1. The sport of boxing should be banned from the Olympic Games because it places athletes at risk and promotes violence among young people.

Scanning

A: The sport of boxing should be banned from the Olympic Games because B: it places athletes at risk **and** promotes violence among young people.

Standardization

Because
B: [Boxing] places athletes at risk.
[and because]
C: [Boxing] promotes violence among young people.
[Thus]
A: The sport of boxing should be banned from the Olympic Games.

13

Diagram

Inductive Argument

2. Because it promotes violence, and because violent sports are not appropriate for international games, the sport of boxing should be banned from the Olympics.

Scanning

<u>Because</u> A: it promotes violence, <u>and because</u> B: violent sports are not appropriate for international games, C: the sport of boxing should be banned from the Olympics.

Standardization

<u>Because</u>

A: [Boxing] promotes violence.

<u>and because</u>

B: Violent sports are not appropriate for international games.

[Thus]

C: The sport of boxing should be banned from the Olympics.

Diagram

Deductive Argument

C. Scan, standardize, and diagram the following arguments.

1. We currently spend less than one-tenth as much protecting ourselves from cyberattacks as we do preventing conventional terrorist attacks. Yet, our military readiness currently depends entirely on the Internet. Banking institutions also rely almost entirely on digital communication with consumers and with one another. It is also true that major transportation systems could be crippled if the Internet went down. So, it is safe to say that the United States is under far greater threat from cyberattacks than from conventional terrorist attacks that employ explosives. It's time to increase our investment in preventing an attack where we are most vulnerable—in critical systems dependent on the Internet.

Scanning

A: We currently spend less than one-tenth as much protecting ourselves from cyberattacks as we do preventing conventional terrorist attacks. <u>Yet</u>, B: our military readiness currently depends entirely on the Internet. C: Banking institutions <u>also</u> rely almost entirely on digital communication with consumers and with one another. <u>It is also true that</u> D: major transportation systems could be crippled if the Internet went down. <u>So</u>, E: it is safe to say that the United States is under far greater threat from cyberattacks than from conventional terrorist attacks that employ explosives. F: It's time to increase our investment in preventing an attack where we are most vulnerable—in critical systems dependent on the Internet.

Standardization

A: We currently spend less than one-tenth as much protecting ourselves from cyberattacks as we do preventing conventional terrorist attacks.

<u>Yet</u>

B: Our military readiness currently depends entirely on the Internet.

<u>[And]</u>

C: Banking institutions also rely almost entirely on digital communication with consumers and with one another.

<u>It is also true that</u>

D: Major transportation systems could be crippled if the Internet went down.

<u>So</u>

E: It is safe to say that the United States is under far greater threat from cyberattacks than from conventional terrorist attacks that employ explosives.

<u>[Thus]</u>

F: It's time to increase our investment in preventing an attack where we are most vulnerable—in critical systems dependent on the Internet.

Diagram

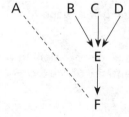

2. Even though opposition to cloning human embryos is heard from some quarters, it is certain that a majority of people will soon support the practice. First, the public will back any research that promises cures to serious, genetically conveyed diseases. Embryo cloning will hasten the eradication of such diseases. In addition, moral objections to human cloning will evaporate because the public will come to understand that cloning embryos does not mean creating human beings in a test tube. Finally, the economic potential of human embryo cloning will provide yet another incentive for broad public acceptance of the technology.

Scanning

<u>Even though</u> A: opposition to cloning human embryos is heard from some quarters, <u>it is certain that</u> B: <u>a majority of Americans will soon support the practice</u>. <u>First</u>, C: the public will back any research that promises cures to serious, genetically conveyed diseases, <u>and</u> D: embryo cloning will hasten the eradication of such diseases. <u>In addition</u>, E: moral objections to human cloning will evaporate <u>because</u> F: the public will come to understand that cloning embryos does not mean creating human beings in a test tube. <u>Finally</u>, G: the economic potential of human embryo cloning will provide yet another incentive for broad public acceptance of the technology.

Standardization

<u>Even though</u>

A: opposition to cloning human embryos is heard from some quarters,

<u>First</u>,

C: The public will support research that promises cures to serious genetically conveyed diseases.

<u>and</u>

D: Embryo cloning will hasten the eradication of such diseases.

<u>In addition, because</u>

F: The public will come to understand that cloning embryos does not mean creating human beings in a test tube.

<u>[Thus,]</u>

E: Moral objections to human cloning will evaporate.

<u>Finally</u>

G: The economic potential of human embryo cloning will provide yet another incentive for broad public acceptance of the technology.

<u>[Therefore]</u>

<u>It is certain that</u>

B: A majority of Americans will soon support [cloning].

Diagram

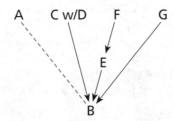

3. Although civil libertarians express concern about the idea, mandatory drug tests should be required of all federal employees. This is because testing would help identify drug abusers, which is crucial to reducing health insurance costs. In addition, testing all federal employees for drugs would provide a good model for private industry to follow.

Scanning

Although A: civil libertarians express concern about the idea, B: mandatory drug tests should be required of all federal employees. This is because C: testing would help identify drug abusers, D: which is crucial to reducing health insurance costs. In addition, E: testing all federal employees for drugs would provide a good model for private industry to follow.

Standardization

Although

A: Civil libertarians express concern about [mandatory drug testing]

This is because

C: Testing would help identify drug abusers

[and because]

D: [Identifying drug abusers] is crucial to reducing health insurance costs.

In addition

E: Testing all federal employees for drugs would provide a good model for private industry to follow.

[Thus]

B: Mandatory drug testing should be required of all federal employees.

Diagram

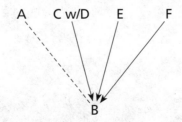

4. Movies portraying acts of violence are consistently among the most financially successful. The violence in many of the most popular new movies, however, develops around the impulse to seek revenge. These same movies connect taking revenge with masculinity. Thus, a cultural definition of masculinity is emerging that incorporates a virtual obligation to do violence to anyone who opposes or offends you. It is also well established that physical violence causes vastly more social problems than it solves, so it is time to develop a new definition of masculinity that recognizes that violent revenge-taking is not a sign of true manhood.

Scanning

A: Movies portraying acts of violence are consistently among the most financially successful. <u>However</u>, B: the violence in many of the most popular new movies develops around the impulse to seek revenge. C: These same movies connect taking revenge with masculinity. <u>Thus</u>, D: a cultural definition of masculinity is emerging that incorporates a virtual obligation to do violence to anyone who opposes or offends you. <u>It is also well established that</u> E: physical violence causes vastly more social problems than it solves. <u>So</u>, F: it is time to develop a new definition of masculinity that recognizes that violent revenge-taking is not a sign of true manhood.

Standardization

A: Movies portraying acts of violence are consistently among the most financially successful.

<u>However,</u>

B: The violence in many of the most popular new movies develops around the impulse to seek revenge.

<u>And</u>

C: These same [popular new] movies connect taking revenge with masculinity.

<u>Thus</u>

D: A cultural definition of masculinity is emerging that incorporates a virtual obligation to do violence to anyone who opposes or offends you.

<u>It is also well established that</u>

E: Physical violence causes vastly more social problems than it solves.

<u>So</u>

F: It is time to develop a new definition of masculinity that recognizes that violent revenge-taking is not a sign of true manhood.

Diagram

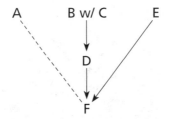

5. The amount of information in the DNA of a single cell bacterium is equivalent to that contained in the *Encyclopedia Britannica*. It is also the case that such a vast amount of information could not have been accumulated as the result of purely random processes, so it is clear that there must have been a designing intelligence behind the creation of life on earth. Therefore, the DNA molecule offers some evidence for the existence of God.

Scanning

A: The amount of information in the DNA of a single cell bacterium is equivalent to that contained in the *Encyclopedia Britannica*. It is also the case that B: such a vast amount of information could not have been accumulated as the result of purely random processes, so it is clear that C: there must have been a designing intelligence behind the creation of life on earth. Therefore, D: the DNA molecule offers some evidence for the existence of God.

Standardization

A: The amount of information in the DNA of a single cell bacterium is equivalent to that contained in the *Encyclopedia Britannica*.

It is also the case that

B: Such a vast amount of information could not have been accumulated as the result of purely random processes.

So it is clear that

C: There must have been a designing intelligence behind the creation of life on earth.

Therefore

D: The DNA molecule offers some evidence for the existence of God.

Diagram

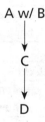

D. Set out the following arguments using Toulmin's model, identifying the data, claim, warrant, and backing for each. If an element is hidden, suggest how it might be stated.

1. A national health care plan is vital, because many people in the United States currently cannot afford adequate health care. When citizens cannot afford a vital service, the government must assist them.

Data	Claim
Many people in the United States currently cannot afford adequate health care.	A national health care plan is vital.

Warrant
When citizens cannot afford a vital service, the government must assist them.

Backing
The values of United States democracy that assign government the role of assisting the citizenry.

2. It is wrong to deny the right to marry to gay people. Such a prohibition violates a fundamental right to seek happiness.

Data	Claim
Many gay people have been denied the right to marry.	It is wrong to deny the right to marry to gay people.

Warrant
Denying the right to marry to gay people violates a fundamental right to seek happiness.

Backing
The principle stated in the Declaration of Independence that everyone has the rights to life, liberty, and the pursuit of happiness.

3. The canyon area ought to be developed, because then more people would have access to it.

Data	Claim
More people then would have access to [a developed canyon area].	The canyon area ought to be developed. |//
Warrant	
What benefits more people is what should be done.	

Backing
A democratic or utilitarian value for pursuing actions that open opportunities to larger numbers of people.

ADDITIONAL EXERCISES

1. Scan, standardize, and diagram the following argument. Draw a wavy line under the argument's conclusion.

   Although the tobacco industry is protesting loudly, the recently implemented tax on cigarettes is a good idea. First, it will help fund the president's new health coverage program. Second, the tax will reduce the number of illnesses related to smoking because it will cause some smokers to quit. Finally, the tax will put special interests on notice that they cannot control health policy.

Scanning

Although A: the tobacco industry is protesting loudly, B: the recently implemented tax on cigarettes is a good idea. First, C: it will help fund the president's new health coverage program. Second, D: the tax will reduce the number of illnesses related to smoking because E: it will cause some smokers to quit. Finally, F: the tax will put special interests on notice that they cannot control health policy.

Standardization

Although

A. The tobacco industry is protesting loudly

First [because]

C. [The tax] will help fund the president's new health coverage program.

Second [because]

E. [The tax] will cause smokers to quit.

D. The tax will reduce the number of illnesses related to smoking.

Finally

F. The tax will put special interests on notice that they cannot control health policy.

[Thus]

B. The recently implemented tax on cigarettes is a good idea.

Diagram

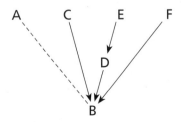

2. What type of proposition is the conclusion of this argument? **proposition of value**

QUIZ

1. Draw a wavy line under the conclusion in each of the following arguments. Scan the arguments. What types of propositions are the conclusions?

   a. Because **A:** it would help identify drug abusers and because **B:** it would eventually reduce health insurance costs, **C:** <u>random drug testing of federal employees should be implemented</u>. In addition, **D:** testing all federal employees for drugs would provide a good model for private industry to follow. **proposition of policy**

   b. Because of **A:** his attention to visual detail and **B:** his command of narrative structure, **C:** <u>Wes Anderson is the best director working today</u>. **proposition of value**

2. Draw a diagram of example a.

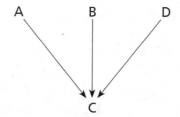

TEST ITEMS

True or False

1. **T** F   When the relationships among terms and conclusions are not clear, standardizing can help clarify them.
2. T **F**   When standardizing an argument, you should leave indefinite references in the original argument as they are.
3. **T** F   Sometimes supplying missing reasons is the only way to really know what someone is arguing.
4. **T** F   Because of the potential for blurring the line between opinion and advocacy, digital advocates must be especially clear about the distinction between an assertion and an argument.
5. **T** F   Inductive arguments move from particular observations to the formulation of general principles or conclusions.
6. **T** F   Complementary reasons must work together to lend support to their conclusion.
7. T **F**   An intermediate conclusion functions as a conclusion, but not as a reason, in an argument.
8. **T** F   A statement is any portion of an argument that has its own function.
9. **T** F   When the cause of an event is well known or generally accepted, we may expect reports or explanations rather than arguments in its support.

10. T **F** When neither side in a controversy wishes to challenge a specific claim, arguments are likely to be advanced.

11. T **F** In the digital age it is no longer necessary for there to be a clear line from evidence to conclusion.

Multiple Choice

1. Identifying and marking the statements in an argument.
    - a. diagramming
    - b. analyzing
    - c. standardizing
    - d. supplying missing premises
    - **e.** scanning

2. Reasons which must work together to lend support to their conclusion.
    - **a.** complementary reasons
    - b. independent reasons
    - c. intermediate conclusions
    - d. conclusions
    - e. linguistic cues

3. Rendering each statement, or implied statement, in the argument as a complete sentence and changing indefinite references such as pronouns to the definite nouns they represent.
    - a. diagramming
    - b. analyzing
    - **c.** standardizing
    - d. supplying missing premises
    - e. scanning

4. Mapping the argument, using only the letters assigned during scanning, and drawing lines from reasons to the conclusions they support.
    - **a.** diagramming
    - b. analyzing
    - c. standardizing
    - d. supplying missing premises
    - e. scanning

5. These arguments move from general principles to specific application of those principles to particular areas.
    - a. inductive arguments
    - **b.** deductive arguments
    - c. complementary reasons
    - d. intermediate conclusions
    - e. diagrams

6. These arguments move from particular observations to the formulation of general principles or conclusions.
    <u>a.</u> inductive arguments
    b. deductive arguments
    c. complementary reasons
    d. intermediate conclusions
    e. diagrams

7. A statement serving as both a conclusion and a reason in an argument.
    a. inductive reason
    b. deductive reason
    c. complementary reason
    <u>d.</u> intermediate conclusion
    e. basic reason

8. Contexts in which arguments are frequently found include:
    a. the need for reasoned support
    b. a controversy
    c. a statement of personal opinion
    <u>d.</u> all of the above
    e. none of the above

9. Stephen Toulmin's term for an argument's conclusion.
    <u>a.</u> claim
    b. warrant
    c. data
    d. backing
    e. qualifier

10. Stephen Toulmin's term for an argument's evidence.
    a. claim
    b. warrant
    <u>c.</u> data
    d. backing
    e. qualifier

11. The text endorses this structure as a means of supplying elements that many be obscure due to the brief or personal tone of a digital message.
    a. inductive argument
    <u>b.</u> Toulmin model
    c. deductive argument
    d. standardization
    e. scanning

Terminology

Provide the term for the following definitions.

1. Identifying and marking the statements in an argument. **scanning**
2. Arguments that move from general principles to specific application of those principles in particular cases. **deductive arguments**
3. Reasons that work together to lend support to their conclusion. **complementary reasons**
4. Arguments that move from particular observations to the formulation of general principles or conclusions. **inductive arguments**
5. Statements that serve as both conclusions and reasons. **intermediate conclusions**
6. Any portion of an argument that has its own function. **statement**
7. Rendering each statement or implied statement in the argument as a complete sentence and changing indefinite references such as pronouns to the definite nouns they represent. **standardizing**
8. Mapping the argument, using only the letters assigned during scanning and drawing lines from reasons to the conclusion they support. **diagramming**
9. Stephen Toulmin's term for a generalization that links data to claim. **warrant**
10. Stephen Toulmin's term for an argument's conclusion. **claim**
11. Stephen Toulmin's term for an argument's evidence. **data**

PART II
The Conditions of Constructive Argumentation

Chapter 4
Ethical Advocacy

EXERCISES

A. Provide an instance of argumentation that you have read or heard about that you consider to be unethical. Explain why you came to this conclusion. Did the individual advancing the argument fail to exhibit a virtue mentioned in this chapter? Should some other principle or virtue of argument ethics be added to those already discussed?

[This assignment works well as a one-page written assignment to be read in class.]

B. Develop your thoughts on argument ethics by answering the following questions:

[Discuss these questions with students in class or have students do a written assignment on one or more of the questions.]

1. For you, what are the most fundamental ethical obligations of individuals presenting or hearing arguments?

2. For you, what constitutes an obvious violation of argumentative ethics?

3. When was the last time you believed you were hearing an unethically presented argument? What about the argument struck you as unethical?

4. Identify four or five values that might garner wide agreement in our own pluralistic society. (A likely example would be the value of freedom of speech.)

5. In what practical ways might an advocate develop the virtues discussed in this chapter as a matter of personal character?

C. Review the discussion of the virtues of an ethical advocate. In light of these virtues, what ethical issues, if any, do the following scenarios raise for you?

[Questions that assist discussion are listed below each scenario.]

1. At a news conference, a member of the press asked a military press officer why the government refused to release film footage of the effects of United States air fire on enemy troops. The footage included violent, graphic images of the effects of machine gun and cannon fire from US planes. The military press officer responded that if such images were released to the press, public support for the war effort would be undermined.

Do citizens of a democracy have a right to access this kind of information?

Is the Pentagon acting unethically by withholding the information?

2. At a school board meeting, a speaker was invited to make a presentation advocating preventing sexually transmitted diseases by distributing condoms in high schools. Angry parents attempted to prevent the presentation by shouting.

Does a speaker have a right to express an unpopular opinion?

Does the audience have an ethical obligation to protect the argumentative context?

3. Members of a group that opposes abortion are distributing materials urging alternatives to women entering an abortion clinic. No physical action is taking place to obstruct entrance to the clinic.

Should these people be allowed to communicate their message in this context?

Is this demonstrating respect for persons?

Is this context one that should be protected for the conduct of arguments?

4. During a campaign speech, a candidate for national political office calls another candidate's moral character into question, based on her alleged misuse of campaign funds. The other candidate is not present to respond.

Is the issue relevant?

Does the public have a legitimate interest in such issues?

5. A proponent of euthanasia has been asked to write an editorial in support of the practice for a news magazine. He believes euthanasia is morally justified in some cases. He also believes that one argument in particular, which he has developed and used several times in public, is both sound and highly persuasive, even to opponents of euthanasia. He decides to show a draft of the editorial to a trusted friend who teaches logic. The friend points out a technical problem in his argument that he had not noticed before. However, the euthanasia advocate believes that his audience would not be able to spot the logical problem in the argument.

Does the end of persuasion justify the means of concealing evidence?

D. Think of an example of a movie, documentary, television program, or song that you feel has a persuasive message. Employing the virtues of advocacy discussed in this chapter, write a one-page paper in which you evaluate your example from an ethical perspective. For example, was courage in advocacy displayed? Honesty? Was the audience treated with regard as reasoning people?

TEST ITEMS

True or False

1. T **F** The effort to change someone's thinking need not be seen as an endeavor with a clear moral dimension.
2. **T** F A framework for thinking about ethical argument is suggested by the three elements: the audience, the topic, and the advocate.
3. T **F** Ethical argumentation may seek to "get around" reason.
4. **T** F Dialogical perspectives in argument ethics focus on attitudes that participants in an argumentative setting hold toward one another.

5. T **F** It is ethical to employ an argument we know to be flawed in our efforts to persuade others, as long as we have a good goal in mind.
6. T **F** Ethical argumentation allows argumentation to continue only as long as both sides are comfortable with the way the argument is progressing.
7. **T** F A virtue is a quality that assists us in making ethically good choices.
8. **T** F Audience members incur some basic ethical responsibilities as they listen to or read arguments.
9. T **F** The controversy that characterizes much public debate is unfortunate and carries with it no benefits.
10. **T** F Ethical virtues, like the virtues of advocacy, are associated with human endeavors such as music or law.

Multiple Choice

1. Ethical perspectives that rely on the essential values of a political system for their criteria of ethical assessment.
    <u>a.</u>   political perspectives
    b.   human nature perspectives
    c.   dialogic perspectives
    d.   situational perspectives
    e.   virtues perspectives

2. Ethical perspectives that identify ethical considerations or principles inherent to each unique communication setting.
    a.   political perspectives
    b.   human nature perspectives
    c.   dialogic perspectives
    <u>d.</u>   situational perspectives
    e.   virtues perspectives

3. The spaces, venues, and relationships in which arguments are made and heard.
    a.   contemporary society
    <u>b.</u>   argumentative contexts
    c.   pluralism
    d.   dialogic ethics
    e.   virtue

4. A term describing the variety of moral and ethical perspectives present in contemporary society.
    a.   ethics
    b.   argumentative context
    <u>c.</u>   pluralism
    d.   dialogic ethics
    e.   virtue

5. Ethical perspectives that elevate efforts to preserve the two-sidedness of public discourse.
    a. ethics
    b. argumentative context
    c. pluralism
    <u>d.</u> dialogic perspectives
    e. virtues perspectives

6. A quality that assists us in making ethically good choices.
    a. situational ethics
    b. argumentativeness
    c. pluralistic thinking
    d. dialogic thinking
    <u>e.</u> a virtue

Terminology

1. The spaces, venues, and relationships in which arguments are made and heard. **argumentative context**

2. The variety of moral and ethical perspectives present in contemporary societies. **pluralism**

3. Ethical perspectives that elevate efforts to preserve the two-sidedness of public discourse. **dialogic perspectives**

4. A quality that assists us in making ethically good choices. **virtue**

5. Ethical perspectives that rely on the essential values of a political system for their criteria of ethical assessment. **political perspectives**

6. Ethical perspectives that identify ethical considerations or principles inherent to each unique communication setting. **situational perspectives**

Short Answer

1. What virtues are identified in the chapter as important to argumentation?
   honesty, courage, cooperation, respect for persons, regard for contexts

2. Why is it important to discuss ethics when studying advocacy in argument?
   Because trying to change another person's thinking is an activity with a clear moral dimension.

3. Identify three benefits of the two-sidedness of controversial argument.
   1. Disagreements are aired.
   2. Ideas are tested.
   3. Positions are refined.

Chapter 5
Reasonable Arguments, Reasonable People

EXERCISES

[The following exercises work well as brief written assignments that can be presented in class.]

A. Think of an argument you have read or heard recently that struck you as particularly unreasonable. Try to identify exactly what seemed unreasonable to you. In which of the five ways discussed in this chapter have you sought to respond to this argument?

   [Like Exercise A in Chapter 4, this assignment works well as a one-page written assignment to be read in class. Another approach is to have students select Exercise A from either Chapter 4 or Chapter 5 and discuss both topics in the same class session.]

B. What is your opinion of Michael Billig's assertion that it is wrong to answer those who question the historicity of the Holocaust? Do you agree that an argument should not be answered in some cases? Why or why not?

C. Would you classify the following example as rebuttal or refutation? Explain your answer.

   1. Governor Rick Snyder of Michigan backs a proposed new $300 million stadium for the Detroit Red Wings on the argument that such a resource would bring needed revenues into downtown Detroit. This idea would make sense if it weren't for the fact that it has already been tried and failed. New stadiums built in the '80s and '90s in Detroit did not generate significant revenue for downtown businesses. People came to the games, then got into their cars and drove home.

   2. Prior to the invasion of Iraq in 2003, some politicians suggested that opposing the invasion was unpatriotic because it meant opposing the president of the United States. Political columnist E. J. Dionne rejected that reasoning. If that were the case, Dionne argued, "then Abraham Lincoln was an unpatriotic appeaser for opposing the Mexican War as a young congressman in the 1840s." [E. J. Dionne Jr., "Patriotic Liberalism," Workingforchange, February 28, 2003, www.workingforchange.com/printitem.cfm?itemid=14574 (Accessed March 1, 2006).]

D. Think of a friend, relative, or acquaintance whom you consider to be particularly reasonable. Describe the qualities of this individual that lead you to this conclusion.

ADDITIONAL EXERCISES

A. Suggest one reasonable argument or appropriate type of evidence to support each of the following statements.

1. As a Roman Catholic, I should not use contraception.

2. Women make fewer comments in business meetings than do their male counterparts.

3. A liberal arts education is better than a technical education.

4. A technical education is better than a liberal arts education.

5. Being sober is better than being drunk.

6. Only law enforcement officers should be allowed to carry handguns.

7. Humans cannot have evolved from the lower species of animals.

8. It seems clear that humans did evolve from lower species of animals.

9. A fetus is (or is not) a living human being with rights.

B. Identify the reason or reasons and the conclusion in each of the following arguments. Then identify a key term in each argument that might have different meanings for different audiences. Suggest two different meanings that might be attached to the terms you have identified.

[Have students discuss their reactions to these claims, as well as possible arguments for and against them. Discuss the question of why reasonable people might disagree on these issues. Students may identify terms other than those listed here as having multiple meanings.]

1. Gays and lesbians are members of a minority group. Thus, accepting them into the military is no different from accepting people of different races. To exclude homosexuals from military service is a form of discrimination.

minority group, discrimination

2. Nuclear power is a safe and economical way of producing energy. The United States should move forward with an aggressive program to develop nuclear power plants in every region of the country.

safe, aggressive

3. Whatever someone wants to believe about God is strictly up to that person, and no other individual has a right to persuade others as to what they ought to believe. Thus, all efforts to proselytize others are wrong.

God, proselytize

4. Some form of censorship should be imposed on popular works of art such as films and television programs, because some images and ideas are too dangerous or immoral to be exhibited.

censorship, immoral

5. The universe contains more than a hundred billion galaxies, and each galaxy contains billions of stars. Astronomers now think that millions of stars in each galaxy have their own planetary systems. This means that it is likely that the universe contains a vast array of intelligent life.

intelligent life

Chapter 5 Reasonable Arguments, Reasonable People

TEST ITEMS

True or False

1. <u>T</u> F It is seldom the case that all of the reasonable arguments are on a single side in a controversy.
2. <u>T</u> F Argument theorist Michael Billig believes that silence may be a reasonable response to some arguments.
3. <u>T</u> F We are not obliged to accept all reasonable arguments.
4. T <u>F</u> Validity is a concern for an argument's evidence.
5. T <u>F</u> A valid argument is, by this criterion alone, a reasonable argument.
6. <u>T</u> F Even when an argument exhibits good evidence, we must also test its validity.
7. T <u>F</u> If an argument has good evidence, then it must also be valid.
8. T <u>F</u> Linguistic consistency is a term describing a concern for an argument's evidence.
9. T <u>F</u> The text takes the position that in most controversies, all the reasonable arguments are on one side.
10. <u>T</u> F The text takes the position that only in rare cases may repudiation be seen as a reasonable response to an argument.
11. <u>T</u> F The things about which we do not ask critical questions are our point of rational vulnerability, the issues about which we are most likely to accept unreasonable arguments.
12. <u>T</u> F Consideration is often a response to new evidence or to an idea important enough to warrant our attention.

Multiple Choice

1. The three criteria of a reasonable argument are:
    <u>a.</u> support, linguistic consistency, validity
    b. ethicality, validity, linguistic consistency
    c. validity, soundness, evidence
    d. persuasiveness, evidence, ethicality
    e. connective, evidence, conclusion

2. Among the possible responses to an argument discussed in the text are:
    a. reaction, rejection, repudiation
    b. acceptance, repudiation, persuasion
    <u>c.</u> acceptance, consideration, rebuttal, repudiation
    d. refutation, deduction
    e. c and d

3. A thoroughly successful rebuttal, one that clearly demonstrates a flaw in the original argument.
    a. repudiation
    b. refutation
    c. rebuttal
    d. reservation
    e. rejection

4. Dismissing an argument without serious consideration.
    a. refutation
    b. rebuttal
    c. reservation
    d. rejection
    e. repudiation

Terminology

A. Provide the correct terms.

1. Identify five possible responses to any argument we read or hear. **acceptance, consideration, rebuttal, refutation, repudiation**

2. A solid structure that allows for reasonable connections between evidence and conclusions in an argument. **validity**

3. A test of a reasonable argument that asks about the strength and accuracy of the evidence it advances to bolster the conclusion. **support**

4. The use of terms in the same way throughout an argument. **linguistic consistency**

5. A counter-argument, a reasoned answer that addresses specific points made or evidence advanced in the original argument. **rebuttal**

6. Dismissing an argument without serious consideration. **repudiation**

B. Distinguish between the definitions of the following pairs of terms.

1. rebuttal / refutation:

A rebuttal is a counter-argument offered in response to an argument. A refutation is a thoroughly successful response, one that clearly demonstrates a damaging flaw to the satisfaction of a relatively objective listener or reader.

2. consideration / acceptance:

Consideration is agreeing to think about an argument further, withholding judgment for the time being, exploring the possibility that it might have merit. Acceptance is adopting the arguer's point of view.

3. support / validity:

Two of the three criteria of a reasonable argument. Support is a concern for the strength and accuracy of the argument's evidence. Validity is a solid internal structure that allows for reasonable connections between evidence and conclusions in an argument.

Short Answer

1. Identify three characteristics of a reasonable person as discussed in the text.

   A reasonable person is:
   1. **Willing to communicate her or his reasons to others.**
   2. **Willing to consider what others have to say.**
   3. **Willing to search for the best reasons and conclusions available.**

2. What three criteria for reasonable arguments are identified in the text?

   support, validity, linguistic consistency

PART III
Support:
The Content of Arguments

Chapter 6
Evaluating Evidence

EXERCISES

A. Using the basic tests discussed in this chapter, identify a potential problem with the evidence in each of the following examples, or in how a critic has applied one or more of the tests discussed in the text.

1. Recent claims that DNA samples prove the existence of Bigfoot are being challenged by independent experts. Although a Texas veterinarian claims to have genetic proof that Bigfoot exists, biologists who have looked at the DNA sample in question claim it comes from an opossum. Asserting that his findings had been published in a scientific journal, reporters and scientists pointed out that the only study to have been published in the journal was the veterinarian's own study.

External inconsistency is the principal problem. Internal inconsistency is an issue in the last sentence as well.

2. It is actually beneficial to your dental health to eat chocolate every day! Recent studies at a major research laboratory have corroborated earlier research proving that regular chocolate consumption prevented dental cavities as effectively as regular tooth brushing.

Accessibility—we do not know whether these laboratories are reliable, whether the companies involved funded the research, how studies were conducted, etc.

3. The US steel industry is under extreme pressure from foreign steel companies that dump their excess production on our market. That is why I am calling for higher trade tariffs on foreign steel as a way to protect trade relationships with countries such as Japan and China. A leading expert on this problem has recently stated that "stiff tariffs on foreign steel imports are the only way to ensure free trade and free markets in this embattled industry."

Internal consistency—the last statement appears to involve a contradiction. "Stiff tariffs" and "free trade and free markets" are at odds.

4. Every year five times as many US citizens die of infections they acquire during a hospitalization than do Canadians—more than seventy thousand Americans as contrasted to fewer than nine thousand Canadians. We should note that Canada also has a socialized medical system, while the United States retains a health-for-profit model. The dramatic disparity in the number of deaths from hospital-acquired infections clearly indicates that it is time for the US to join the rest of the world and turn the administration of our medical system over to the government.

The most obvious problem is relevance—the fact of socialization is not connected to preventing hospital-acquired infections in any clear way.

5. Because of the tremendous potential benefits of embryonic stem cell research, we need to proceed immediately with an aggressive research program that allows use of new sources of embryonic stem cells in research. Because significant dangers are associated with such research, current legislation allows for experimentation only on government-approved stem cell lines. It is my view that the current laws should remain in place until adequate safeguards are established for embryonic stem cells. These safeguards may take years to develop.

Internal consistency—self-contradictory claims are advanced.

6. "The widely cited statistic that one in three women ages 35 to 39 will not be pregnant after a year of trying, for instance, is based on an article published in 2004 in the journal *Human Reproduction*. Rarely mentioned is the source of the data: French birth records from 1670 to 1830. The chance of remaining childless—30 percent—was also calculated based on historical populations. In other words, millions of women are being told when to get pregnant based on statistics from a time before electricity, antibiotics, or fertility treatment." [Jean Twenge, "How Long Can You Wait to Have a Baby?," *The Atlantic,* July/August 2013, http://www.theatlantic.com/magazine/archive/2013/07/how-long-can-you-wait-to-have-a-baby/309374/ (Accessed August 5, 2013).]

As the rebuttal indicates, recency is the most obvious problem with the initial argument. Accessibility of the original study is also an issue for this evidence.

B. Explain how the test of external consistency has been employed in each of the following examples. Identify at least one difference regarding the assertion of inconsistency in the example.

1. Initial reports by journalists following the 2005 floods in New Orleans indicated those who died were disproportionately black and poor. However, a study of the list of the dead released by Louisiana state officials indicates that neither claim is true. The percentages of victims who were black or below the poverty level do not differ markedly from averages in the city. The death figures do show that the victims were disproportionately elderly. Of those who died in Hurricane Katrina's aftermath, 74 percent were 60 years old or older, while only 15 percent of the city's population is in that age range.

The study contradicts initial reports.

2. Executives at large search engines and social networking organizations claimed to have been unaware the government was gathering personal information from their computers, but security experts countered that large-scale data mining operations could not have taken place without corporate knowledge, indeed, cooperation. While it is possible the executives themselves were unaware of efforts to spy on private citizens, some employees had to have known. Indeed, so complex and powerful are the security measures that companies such as Google and Facebook employ, it would not be possible for an outside entity to collect, let alone decipher, sensitive personal data on users of these services without inside assistance.

Other available evidence contradicts what the executives have said.

Chapter 6   Evaluating Evidence

TEST ITEMS

True or False

1. <u>T</u> F   Good evidence should be consistent with the best of other available evidence.
2. T <u>F</u>   Evidence is internally consistent when it is not at odds with evidence from other sources.
3. T <u>F</u>   If we are inclined to question the evidence advanced in an argument, it is not important that the evidence be accessible to us.
4. <u>T</u> F   When an argument advances a questionable claim, and when the evidence for the claim is unavailable in the argument or the evidence's sources are unknown or inaccessible, we are under no obligation to accept the argument.
5. T <u>F</u>   When we are assessing the adequacy of the evidence in an argument, the seriousness of the question being decided becomes irrelevant.
6. T <u>F</u>   When we are testing the recency of evidence, the issue at hand is not an important consideration.
7. <u>T</u> F   To qualify a source is to state the source's credentials or give reasons for its credibility.
8. T <u>F</u>   The test of relevance asks whether evidence is available to us for scrutiny.
9. <u>T</u> F   Though evidence usually originates in experience, we always view it through the lenses of our personal values.
10. <u>T</u> F   The test of internal consistency asks whether the evidence contradicts itself.

Terminology

1. The availability of evidence for examination. **accessibility**
2. Whether the evidence, when taken together, is sufficient to support its claim. **adequacy**
3. The requirement that evidence must not contradict itself. **internal consistency**
4. Stating the source's credentials or giving reasons for its credibility. **qualifying the source**
5. Whether the evidence advanced has any bearing on the argument's conclusion. **relevance**
6. The test of evidence that asks whether the evidence is up-to-date. **recency**
7. The test of evidence that asks whether the evidence is sharply at odds with the majority or the best evidence from other sources. **external consistency**

Short Answer

1. In what cases is interpretation of evidence important?

    When evidence is technical, difficult to understand, or obscure.

    When evidence might be taken several ways.

    When the evidence's implications might not be readily appreciated.

2. Provide four general tests of evidence discussed in this chapter.

    1. Is the evidence internally consistent?

    2. Is the source of the evidence credible?

    3. Is the evidence externally consistent?

    4. Is the evidence accessible?

    5. Is the evidence adequate to support the conclusion?

    6. Is the evidence recent enough?

    7. Is the evidence relevant to the conclusion?

3. What is the difference between internal and external consistency of evidence?

    Internal consistency has to do with whether the source contradicts itself.

    External consistency asks whether a source is generally consistent with the best available evidence from other sources.

Chapter 7
Locating and Evaluating Sources of Evidence

EXERCISES

A. Compare the coverage of a major event or controversy by two US news magazines. Is one publication more conservative or liberal in its coverage of the story than is the other? What evidence did you find of a political perspective?

  [Have students provide specific criteria to support their judgments.]

B. Compare the coverage of the two periodicals in exercise A to that offered by some alternative press publication—for example, *The Progressive, Mother Jones,* or *The Utne Reader*—on the same topic. What differences do you see between the coverage in these publications and the coverage in the mainstream publications?

C. Locate an editorial or news report on a similar or related topic in a newspaper or news magazine originating in another country. Examples, in addition to sources mentioned in this chapter, include the French newspaper *Le Monde* and the British newspaper *The Guardian.* You might also consult a newspaper whose audience is made up of members of a particular ethnic or language group, such as *The Arab Times.* What differences in emphasis and coverage do you notice when you compare these with United States sources?

TEST ITEMS

True or False

1. T <u>F</u> Scholarly journals are often good sources of very reliable evidence, and their language and style of writing make them easy for most readers to use.

2. T <u>F</u> The stories or reports in general interest periodicals are written by qualified experts.

3. <u>T</u> F Determining the recency of a book is usually as simple as checking the publication date.

4. <u>T</u> F A writer's efforts to discredit a group by the use of a label is often a good clue as to that writer's political orientation.

5. T <u>F</u> Because everyone's writing is informed by assumptions, when you are ascertaining a source's political perspective it is not helpful to ask what assumptions seem to be at work in the writing.

6. T <u>F</u> As books may be read by anyone, it is not important to ask about the audience for which a book was written.

7. <u>T</u> F   Television documentary programs are influenced by pressures from donors and sponsoring organizations.
8. <u>T</u> F   Among the first markers of a reliable web site are its language and appearance.

Multiple Choice

1. *Psychological Bulletin* and *Journal of the American Medical Association* are examples of
    a. special-interest periodicals
    <u>b.</u> scholarly journals
    c. popular magazines
    d. tabloids
    e. professional bulletins

2. Which of the following is not recommended in the text as a question to ask when evaluating a book as a source?
    a. Who wrote the book?
    b. When was the book published?
    c. Who is the book's publisher?
    d. Does the author have an evident bias?
    <u>e.</u> None of the above: These are all questions that should be asked when you are evaluating a book as a source of evidence.

3. Which of the following questions did the text recommend as helpful in ascertaining a source's political perspective?
    a. For whom did the source vote in the last election?
    <u>b.</u> What assumptions seem to be at work in the writing?
    c. What political organizations sponsor the source?
    d. all of the above
    e. b and c

4. In evaluating an Internet site it is important to ask:
    a. Who created the site?
    b. What do the language and appearance suggest about the site?
    c. For what audience was the site intended?
    d. Is the site's evidence accessible?
    <u>e.</u> All of the above are important questions to ask when evaluating an Internet site.

Short Answer

1. List any four questions discussed in the text that can be asked when evaluating a book as a source of evidence.

   1. Who wrote the book?
   2. When was the book published?
   3. Who is the book's publisher?
   4. For what kind of audience was the book written?
   5. Does the author have an evident bias?
   6. What method of obtaining data or conducting research did the book's author use?
   7. What do others think of the source?

2. Provide any three questions or considerations the text suggests for ascertaining a source's political perspective.

   1. What assumptions seem to be at work?
   2. Imagine the event in question being reported by a different group.
   3. Consider the reputation of the source.
   4. How are groups described or treated?
   5. What style and language are used?

Terminology

1. The careful review of submitted research reports. **the editorial process**

2. Periodicals that focus on a specific topic but are written for a wider audience than are scholarly journals. **special-interest periodicals**

Chapter 8
Using Statistics as Evidence

EXERCISES

A. For each of the following generalizations, identify (a) the sample, (b) the finding, (c) the population, (d) the property, and (e) the extent.

1. A telephone survey of 500 Democrats who voted in the last election indicated that 75 would now vote for a Republican candidate. Thus, at least 15 percent of Democrats will switch to the Republican Party in the next election.

Sample: 500 Democrats

Finding: 75 would now vote for a Republican candidate

Population: Democrats (taken from generalizing statement in second sentence)

Property: will switch to the Republican party

Extent: at least 15 percent

2. Most Americans oppose continued United States military involvement in the Middle East. A recent poll of 250 people living in or around Chicago revealed that 63 percent of those surveyed oppose such involvement.

Sample: 250 people living in or around Chicago

Finding: 63 percent of those surveyed opposed US involvement in the Middle East.

Population: Americans

Property: opposing continued United States involvement in the Middle East

Extent: most

3. A survey commissioned by the American Bar Association Young Lawyers' Division asked a random sample of over 3,000 attorneys to rate their level of job satisfaction. A surprising 25 percent said they were either somewhat or very dissatisfied with their work. Thus, a substantial minority of attorneys is not happy with having chosen a career in the law.

Sample: 3,000 attorneys

Finding: 25 percent said they were either somewhat or very dissatisfied with their work.

Population: attorneys

Property: not being happy with having chosen a career in the law

Extent: a substantial minority

4. A 2005 Associated Press/Ipsos poll surveyed 1,000 adult Americans. The poll found that 70 percent of those surveyed were worried about the federal deficit. However, the same poll also found that only 35 percent of those surveyed were willing to make a personal financial sacrifice to balance the budget. Thus, a sweeping majority of us is concerned about the deficit, while a minority of people is willing to adjust lifestyles to make a difference. (Note: There are two findings, two extents, and two properties in this example.)

Sample: 1,000 adult Americans

Findings: "70 percent of those surveyed were worried about the federal deficit" and "35 percent of those surveyed were willing to make a present sacrifice to balance the budget"

Population: us (adult Americans seems to be assumed)

Properties: "being concerned about the deficit" and "being willing to adjust their lifestyles to make a difference"

Extents: "a sweeping majority" and "a minority"

5. A random sample of 1,500 graduating high school seniors from different regions of the country indicated that less than one-third consider the United States space program to be an important government priority. Therefore, a small minority of the rising generation of US voters will be willing to provide support for the very costly venture of continued space exploration.

Sample: 1,500 graduating high school seniors from different regions of the country

Finding: less than one-third consider the United States space program to be an important government priority

Population: the rising generation of US voters

Property: being willing to provide support for space exploration

Extent: a small minority

6. A survey of California residents indicates that a vast majority are unhappy with the state's current direction. In a survey of 1500 registered voters, 80 percent responded with "agree" or "strongly agree" to the statement: California is on the wrong track.

Sample: 1,500 registered voters

Finding: 80 percent responded with "agree" or "strongly agree" to the statement: California is on the wrong track

Population: California residents

Property: being unhappy with the state's current direction

Extent: a vast majority

B. In the following examples, differentiate between the statistical evidence and any conclusion based on those statistics.

1. Following a recent Right to Life rally in Washington, DC, the United States Parks Department estimated the number of people in attendance at 200,000. Organizers of the march estimated the number at 500,000, **and charged the Parks Department with capitulating to pressure from the media and the pro-choice movement to underestimate the numbers.**

2. The figures just in for April show that new home sales dropped 9.5 percent to an annual rate of 894,000. In March, economists had projected an annual new home sales rate of 988,000. This is the biggest decline in percentage since 1997. **The figures, combined with a higher jobless rate and the drop in the stock market, may point to a significant downturn in the economy.** Government economists argue, however, that despite the apparent decline, new home sales are actually up 0.6 percent when compared to the projection of 889,000 in April. **These economists maintain that we should not be alarmed by a single number.**

3. During the first quarter of this year, business investment in equipment purchases, computer equipment included, decreased at an annual rate of 2.6 percent. Business equipment purchases also declined the last quarter of last year. **We have to consider these drops to be the "canary in the mine" for our economy. Businesses aren't investing in equipment, so they must be projecting a stagnant economy.**

4. Historical studies show that 15,000 people have been executed in the United States in the last 300 years. **This statistic gives us a strong reason to believe that the human race is self-destructive.**

5. The latest census data reveal that, for the first time since census figures have been recorded, the non-Hispanic white population in California dropped below 50 percent of the state's total population. **This fact accounts for a well-funded lobbying organization's inability to get popular support for a proposal banning bilingual education in public schools.**

ADDITIONAL EXERCISES

A. Identify any evident problems in the following generalizations.

1. Increasingly, teachers in the United States are unhappy with their work. Of 112 veteran teachers interviewed, 87 said they found teaching less rewarding and more stressful than when they entered the occupation.

The sample is clearly too small to allow a generalization to such a large group. Moreover, careful efforts at stratification would have to be evident to support a generalization about such a diverse group. For example, the study does not appear to account for newer teachers.

2. Few investors are seeking professional advice about investments. Responses from 377 members of the 90,000-member American Investors Association suggest that about 70 percent of investors already do their own investment research, never consulting a professional.

It is not clear that the sample is large enough or random enough to support the generalization. We would need to know about stratification across groups such as small investors, large investors, experienced investors, and so on.

B. What problem is evident in these directions to survey respondents?

We are requesting that you complete the enclosed survey, which will provide Citizens Against Drugs with important information about how Americans feel about drug use and random drug testing in the workplace. Before you fill out the survey, however, you should realize that more than 14,000,000 Americans have admitted using drugs this month alone, and 1 in 6 admit they use drugs at work! You also should realize that no comprehensive law requires random drug testing of our nation's workers! Transportation workers, health workers, and employees of the food industries all use drugs at work on a regular basis, and they are getting away with it! Please take five or six minutes to give us your opinion about this dangerous situation.

Respondents are essentially told how to respond to the survey.

QUIZ

1. For the following generalization, identify the elements requested:

   Well over half of the 35 million elderly citizens in the United States oppose investing Social Security funds in the stock market. Of 1,900 Americans over the age of 64 responding to a recent telephone survey, 57 percent said they were opposed or strongly opposed to this idea.

   Sample: 1,900 Americans over the age of 64

   Population: 35 million elderly citizens in the United States

   Property: being opposed to investing Social Security funds in the stock market

   Extent: well over half

   Finding: 57 percent of 1,900 Americans over the age of 64 were opposed or strongly opposed to investing Social Security funds in the stock market

TEST ITEMS

True or False

1. <u>T</u> F   Knowing the extent of the generalization is important to rendering a judgment about how well a sample supports a generalization.
2. <u>T</u> F   Sometimes a "mean" can be a misleading figure, especially when we take "average" as meaning "usual" or "typical."
3. <u>T</u> F   It is a good idea to be careful about accepting means reported on their own.
4. <u>T</u> F   A generalization is reasonable only to the extent that the assertion expressed in its connective—the sample represents the population—is accurate.
5. T <u>F</u>   Generalization arguments seldom move beyond their actual evidence in reaching their conclusions.
6. <u>T</u> F   A sample must be large enough to account for all of the variance in a population, but usually no larger.
7. T <u>F</u>   A "random" sample is one gathered in an unplanned way: literally, at random.

Chapter 8 Using Statistics as Evidence   53

8. <u>T</u> F A sample of a population must represent the diverse elements in the population in order to be representative.
9. <u>T</u> F Generalizing from a sample is a form of inductive reasoning.
10. T <u>F</u> In sampling, the rule governing size is to get the biggest sample possible.
11. <u>T</u> F Some statistics are the result of record-keeping rather than statistical sampling.
12. T <u>F</u> For some statistics, the reliability of the source is insignificant.
13. <u>T</u> F Relative differences among members of a population are referred to as variation.
14. T <u>F</u> A stratified sample is one that is chosen at random.
15. <u>T</u> F Some statistical interpretations are advanced to support predictions.

Multiple Choice

1. Observed members of a group that are taken to be representative of the whole group.
    a. generalization
    b. extent
    <u>c.</u> sample
    d. property
    e. induction

2. That portion of the population that is said in the generalization to exhibit the property.
    a. generalization
    <u>b.</u> extent
    c. sample
    d. property
    e. induction

3. A quality projected from the sample to the population in a generalization.
    a. finding
    b. extent
    c. sample
    <u>d.</u> property
    e. induction

4. What was discovered about members of a sample as the result of a survey or study.
    <u>a.</u> finding
    b. extent
    c. sample
    d. property
    e. induction

5. The most common observation or response in a sample or survey.
    a. average
    b. median
    c. mean
    d. bias
    e. *mode*

6. The average, or the sum of a set of figures divided by the number of figures in the set.
    a. mode
    b. median
    c. *mean*
    d. bias
    e. average

7. The figure that divides the top half from the bottom half in a range of figures.
    a. mode
    b. *median*
    c. mean
    d. bias
    e. average

8. A sample in which every member of the population had an equal chance of being selected.
    a. large sample
    b. stratified sample
    c. *random sample*
    d. biased sample
    e. adequate sample

9. A sample that adequately reflects the groups within the population.
    a. large sample
    b. skewed sample
    c. random sample
    d. *stratified sample*
    e. adequate sample

Terminology

Provide the correct term for each of the following definitions.

1. In a generalization, the members of a group actually observed or consulted.
sample

2. Claims that take, as their evidence, observation of a sample drawn from a population, and advance a general conclusion about members of the population not directly observed. **generalizations**

3. The group or class to which the generalization is meant to apply. **population**

4. A quality projected from the sample to the population. **property**

5. In a generalization from a sample, that portion of the population that is said to exhibit the property. **extent**

6. The most common observation or response in a sample or survey. **mode**

7. Average, or the sum of a set of figures divided by the number of figures in the set. **mean**

8. The figure that exactly divides the top half from the bottom half in a range of figures. **median**

9. The total number of individuals in the sample. **sample size**

10. A sample in which every member of a given population had an equal opportunity of being selected for the sample. **random sample**

Short Answer

1. Provide the connective that links the evidence of the sample to the conclusion in a generalization.

    The sample represents the population.

2. Provide three tests of the accuracy of the claim that the sample represents the population in a descriptive generalization.

    1. Is the sample of sufficient size to represent the population?

    2. Is the sample random?

    3. Is the sample stratified?

3. Identify two factors important to determining whether a sample is of sufficient size.

    1. the size of the population

    2. the likelihood that members of the population will resemble each other

4. Differentiate between the meanings of the following pairs of terms:

    a. random sample / stratified sample

    A random sample is selected in a manner allowing every member of the population equal chance of inclusion. A stratified sample accounts for groups within the population.

    b. sample / population

    The sample is the group observed. The population is the group from which the sample was drawn and about which the generalization is advanced.

Application

A. For each of the following generalizations, identify the sample, finding, population, extent, and property.

1. A survey of 148 officer candidates at West Point Academy indicates that more than 80 percent of future military leaders in the United States are more inclined toward the use of diplomacy than of military force. Thus, it is clear that most military leaders of tomorrow will be more prepared to talk than to fight.

Sample: 148 officer candidates at West Point Academy

Finding: 80 percent of officer candidates are more inclined toward use of diplomacy than force

Population: military leaders of tomorrow

Property: being more prepared to talk than to fight

Extent: most

2. I have spoken with over a thousand younger voters all across the country, many of whom express growing anxiety for the environment. Thus, a majority of our young people are deeply concerned about the environment.

Sample: over a thousand younger voters all across the country

Finding: many younger voters express growing anxiety for the environment

Population: young people

Property: being deeply concerned about the environment.

Extent: a majority

Chapter 9
Using Testimony as Evidence

EXERCISES

A. Which of the following are examples of expert testimony and which of lay testimony? When is concurrent testimony being advanced? Indicate whether the sources should be considered biased, unbiased, or reluctant.

1. "The increasing use of active sonar by militaries around the world threatens the survival of numerous marine species, including entire populations of whales and porpoises," according to Frederick O'Reagan, president of the International Fund for Animal Welfare, an animal rights organization that has been heavily involved with efforts to protect sea mammals from the effects of marine technology. ["European Parliament Calls for Halt to High Intensity Naval Sonar Use," Natural Resource Defense Fund, October 2004, http://www.nrdc.org/media/pressreleases/041028a.asp (Accessed October 9, 2006).]

expert, individual, biased testimony

2. A local high school has had problems with students getting sick during classes. Some teachers suspect that a newly installed insulation material may be causing the symptoms, which include headaches, nausea, and coughing. After sampling the air in the classrooms, two environmental toxicologists hired by the school board, with the consent of the teachers' union, testified that "the insulation in the school building is safe and could not be causing the sicknesses."

These concurrent, expert sources are likely to be unbiased. The fact that they are "hired by the school board" and "with the consent of the teachers' union" suggests an effort has been made to secure unbiased sources.

3. You testify in court that a recently deceased eccentric millionaire signed a note leaving you $6 million after you helped him to change a flat tire that had stranded him in a Nevada desert.

lay, biased, individual testimony

4. Three independent handwriting experts, called by the court and not associated with clients on either side of the case, testify in court that a recently deceased eccentric millionaire signed a note leaving you $6 million.

expert, unbiased, concurrent testimony

5. Daniel Freeman of the Institute of Psychiatry at University College London says that the number of paranoid people is increasing every year. Freeman states that one in four members of the general public has paranoid thoughts on a regular basis. "These days, we daren't let our children play outside. We're suspicious of strangers. Security cameras are everywhere." [Rosie Mestrel, "Paranoid? Me? Who Said So?" *Los Angeles Times,* October 21, 2008, http://latimesblogs.latimes.com/booster_shots/2008/10/paranoid-me-who.html (Accessed July 30, 2009).]

expert, individual, unbiased

6. Several followers of a faith healer testify that they have seen him heal people with terminal illnesses.

lay, concurrent, biased (Because the leader of these concurrent lay witnesses stands to have his reputation enhanced by their testimony; this would be considered biased testimony.)

7. A recent report from ACT indicated that "only about half of this year's high school students have the reading skills they need to succeed in college, and even fewer are prepared for college-level science and math courses . . . ." Richard L. Ferguson, chief executive of ACT, said: "It is very likely that hundreds of thousands of [high school] students will have a disconnect between their plans for college and the cold reality of their preparation for college." [Tamar Lewin, "Many Going to College Aren't Ready, Report Finds," *The New York Times,* August 17, 2005, A13.]

expert, individual, unbiased (Ferguson works professionally with standardized tests, but has no clear interest in how this testimony is received.)

8. Professor Noel Sharkey of the University of Sheffield's Department of Computer Science will speak to a group of international leaders in May. His topic is the increasing use of fully autonomous weapons in battle. The so-called "killer robots" are redefining warfare and introducing new risks to civilian populations. "If we do not put an end to this trend for automating warfare . . . ," he says, "we could face a very bleak future where machines are delegated with the decision to kill humans." ["Robotics Experts to Debate 'Killer Robots' Policies at UN," May 13, 2014, *Kurzweil Accelerating Intelligence,* http://www.kurzweilai.net/robotics-experts-to-debate-killer-robots-policies-at-un#!prettyPhoto (Accessed May 16, 2014).]

Expert, individual, apparent bias. A bias in his testimony depends on whether Sharkey wishes to keep his field of study—computer science—free of the moral concerns over computerized weapons systems. His use of phrases such as "put an end to this trend," "bleak future," and "delegated with the decision to kill humans," suggest that he is not neutral on the topic.

9. A widely respected reporter for a major newspaper writes an editorial column critical of the paper's decision to install a caller ID phone system. Such a system allows the paper to identify all callers to the newspaper and thus, according to the reporter, "compromises reporting by violating the crucial principle of source anonymity."

expert, individual, reluctant

10. Richard Schmidt, a psychologist who works as an auto industry consultant, is an expert on human motor skills. Schmidt argues that the problem of sudden acceleration is typically caused by drivers: "When the driver says they have their foot on the brake, they are . . . wrong. The human motor system is not perfect, and it doesn't always do what it is told." [Ken Bensinger and Ralph Vartabedian, "Data Point to Toyota's Throttles, Not Floor Mats," *Los Angeles Times*, November 29, 2009, http://mobile.latimes.com/inf/infomo?view=webarticle&feed:a=latimes_1min&feed:c=nationnews&feed:i=50753295&nopaging=1 (Accessed March 31, 2010).]

expert, individual, biased (The witness is someone working as a consultant for the auto industry, and is finding the industry not to be at fault.)

TEST ITEMS

True or False

1. T **F** Testimony from a reluctant source will always be reliable.
2. T **F** Expertise can be transferred from one arena to another.
3. T **F** Testimony from individuals who will lose something as a result of their testimony being accepted is called biased testimony.
4. **T** F Audiences usually presume that testimony is less reliable when it conflicts with other testimony.
5. **T** F Lay or ordinary testimony is a report of personal observation, experience, or opinion on a topic not requiring special expertise.
6. T **F** Lay testimony should be used where technical knowledge is important to resolving an issue.
7. **T** F We tend to assume that people do not readily testify against their self interest.
8. **T** F When evaluating expert testimony, our greatest concern is the expert's qualifications to testify.
9. **T** F In building a case, writers and speakers often combine expert and lay testimony.
10. T **F** Testimony that is consistent with other available sources of testimony on a topic is called independent testimony.

Multiple Choice

1. The reported observations, experience, or opinions of others, not requiring special expertise.

    <u>a.</u> lay testimony
    b. testimonial evidence
    c. biased source
    d. unbiased source
    e. expert testimony

2. A source who stands to gain if his or her testimony is accepted.

    a. unbiased source
    b. reluctant source
    <u>c.</u> biased source
    d. concurrent source
    e. none of the above

3. A source who stands to lose if his or her testimony is accepted.

    a. unbiased source
    <u>b.</u> reluctant source
    c. biased source
    d. concurrent source
    e. none of the above

4. A source who stands neither to lose or to gain if his or her testimony is accepted.

    <u>a.</u> unbiased source
    b. reluctant source
    c. biased source
    d. concurrent source
    e. none of the above

5. When using testimony as evidence, it is a good idea to:

    a. quote sources accurately
    b. identify your sources
    c. be brief
    d. a and b
    <u>e.</u> all of the above

Terminology

1. Personal reports about direct experiences, expression of personal opinion, or judgment based on expert knowledge. **testimony**

2. Testimony from individuals who stand to gain if what they say is accepted. **biased testimony**

3. Testimony from individuals with no particular interest in how their testimony is received. **unbiased testimony**

4. Testimony that is consistent with other available sources of testimony on the topic. **concurrent testimony**

5. The judgment or opinion of a qualified specialist in a discipline about matters relevant to that discipline. **expert testimony**

6. Testimony from sources who stand to lose something as a result of their testimony. **reluctant testimony**

Short Answer

1. Provide a special test of expert testimony discussed in the text.

   Does the individual have credentials as an expert in the appropriate field?

2. Provide four guidelines discussed in the text for using testimony.

   1. Quote sources accurately.

   2. Qualify the source.

   3. Identify your sources.

   4. Avoid biased sources

   5. Use qualified sources.

   6. Be brief.

3. Provide any two of the three specific uses of expert testimony outlined in the text.

   1. To explain a complex problem.

   2. To sum up the significance of a problem.

   3. To support a proposed solution to a problem.

PART IV
Validity:
The Structure of Arguments

Chapter 10
Validity in Conditional and Enumeration Arguments

EXERCISES

A. For each of the following conditional arguments, indicate which statement serves as the conditional statement, which as the second reason, and which as the conclusion. Put the conditional statement in its "if-then" form if necessary. State whether the argument affirms or denies its antecedent or consequent. Indicate whether the argument is valid or invalid.

[Some terms that help identify when an idea is being affirmed or denied have been underlined.]

1. If our administrators were well trained, then our schools would be among the best. Our schools are not among the best, so our administrators must not be well trained.

Conditional statement: If our administrators were well trained, then our schools would be among the best.

Second reason: Our schools <u>are not among the best</u>,

Conclusion: so our administrators must not be well trained.

denies the consequent, valid

2. Local government will not improve unless people get involved. People are getting more involved, so I'm sure we'll see improvements.

Local government will not improve unless people get involved.

Conditional statement becomes: If people do not get involved, local government will not improve.

Second reason: People <u>are getting more involved</u>,

Conclusion: so I'm sure we'll see improvements.

denies the antecedent, invalid

3. The government said it would intervene only if problems arose in the region. Problems arose, so the government intervened.

The government said it would intervene only if problems arose in the region.

[Conditional statement becomes: If problems do not arise in the region, the government says it will not intervene.]

Second reason: <u>Problems arose</u>,

Conclusion: so the government intervened.

invalid, denies the antecedent

[Ask students how this argument might be made valid by a different second reason, e.g., There were <u>not</u> problems, so we did not intervene.]

4. If this is a genuine Picasso, it will exhibit his careful attention to form. It does exhibit such careful attention to form, so it must be a genuine work of the master.

Conditional statement: If this is a genuine Picasso, it will exhibit his careful attention to form.

Second reason: It does exhibit such careful attention to form,

Conclusion: so it must be a genuine work of the master.

invalid, affirms the consequent

[This argument is not saying that <u>only</u> Picasso will show attention to form, but that <u>all</u> of his paintings will exhibit such attention.]

5. We know that when food supplies are short in the southern part of a country, the residents flee to the north. Food supplies now are quite short in the south, so we can expect a crush of refugees to the north within the month.

Conditional statement: We know that when [if] food supplies are short in the southern part of a country, [then] the residents flee to the north.

Second reason: Food supplies now are quite short in the south,

Conclusion: so we can expect a crush of refugees to the north within the month.

valid, affirms the antecedent

B. Each example in this exercise is a dilemma, an enumeration argument, or an argument from direction. Identify the type of argument advanced in each of the following.

1. Giving loans to Third World countries leaves them with a crippling debt that they never can pay off. The effort to pay off interest on the debt leads to further borrowing and deeper debt. The lending nations are left with bad debts. Their economies suffer as a result. Thus, it would be better not to make loans to Third World countries. **argument from direction**

2. A nation's value system can be derived from one of three sources: a common religion, a general culture, or a unifying statement of citizen rights. The United States has not had a common religion for a long time and we no longer can claim to have a culture common to most of our citizens. Thus, the Constitution remains our only source for common, unifying values. **enumeration argument**

3. It is not abortion itself that I oppose but, rather, the principle it introduces. It legitimizes the notion that a society can terminate unwanted human life. This principle, once accepted, can be extended and applied to a wide variety of potentially "unwanted" human life. The aged, the terminally ill, the handicapped—in another time, perhaps even members of a despised race or religious faith—all these people are at risk. **argument from direction**

4. It costs $32,000 a year to keep a prisoner in prison, and $4,000 to manage the same prisoner on probation. Thus, though releasing criminals is unpopular with voters, it is more cost-effective than simply keeping them in prison for long periods of time. **dilemma**

5. Macroevolution—evolution from one species to another—has never been observed, nor has it been produced by natural mutations, nor by induced mutations. Macroevolution, therefore, is not scientifically verifiable. **enumeration argument**

6. Darwin scholar John Campbell points out that in *On the Origin of Species,* Charles Darwin argues that "either the evidence he has presented indicates evolution is the known law of creation or God is the author of deceit" by making it appear in nature that evolution occurs. [John Angus Campbell, "Darwin, Thales, and the Milkmaid," in *Perspectives on Argumentation: Essays in Honor of Wayne Brockriede,* ed. Robert Trapp and Janice Schuetz (Prospect Park, Ill: Waveland, 1990), 207–220.] **dilemma**

C. Are the following disjunctive arguments valid? Explain your answers, making reference to the disjuncts as either inclusive or exclusive.

1. Either Jones will have his contract renewed or he will look for a new job. He is looking for a new job, so his contract must not have been renewed.

invalid, affirms an inclusive disjunct

2. Either Ms. Garcia has forgotten the rules or she is deliberately trying to usurp the committee's authority. She is fully aware of what the rules require in these cases, so this is a deliberate attempt to circumvent the committee.

valid, denies an inclusive disjunct ("She is fully aware" means she has *not* forgotten.)

3. The planet's rings are formed of either rock or ice, and cannot be formed of both substances. We have no way of testing for ice using spectrography, but we can test for rock. Using this test we have discovered that the rings do consist of rock, so they must not be made up of ice.

valid, affirms an exclusive disjunct

4. Because of the size of the city's financial burden, the only possibilities for avoiding bankruptcy are to reduce retiree benefits or to cut back on emergency services. We have decided that cutting retiree benefits is not fair to the thousands of retirees affected, so emergency services will be cut.

The argument is valid because it denies a disjunct, and the disjuncts are not exclusive.

D. Each of the following exhibits the same problem of enumerative reasoning discussed in this chapter. Identify the problem and explain how each argument might be answered.

1. Either we decide what the future of our nation will be by enacting strict immigration laws, or illegal immigration will decide that future for us.

2. Will you sign our petition supporting animal rights, or are you in favor of abusing animals?

Each example represents a false dilemma that unreasonably limits the available options, when other options could easily be provided.

68 Part IV Validity: The Structure of Arguments

ADDITIONAL EXERCISES

A. For each of the following, state whether A is a necessary or sufficient condition for B.

1. A. Having a radio **[is necessary for]**
   B. Having an FM Radio

2. A. Being a father **[is sufficient for]**
   B. Being male

3. A. Eating wheat cereal **[is sufficient for]**
   B. Eating a grain product

4. A. Being in a building **[is necessary for]**
   B. Being in a skyscraper

B. Put the following two items in standard form and test validity.

1. If a child has not had enough sleep, the child will become fussy. This child's fussiness, thus, results from a lack of sleep.

If a child has not had enough sleep, then the child will become fussy.

This child is fussy.

Thus

This child has not had enough sleep.

Affirms the consequent: invalid.

2. If you complete college, you will be likely to achieve a high standard of living. Bill has not completed college, so he will not achieve a high standard of living.

If you complete college, then you will be likely to achieve a high standard of living.

Bill has not completed college.

So

[Bill] will not achieve a high standard of living.

Denies the antecedent: Invalid.

3. What two valid arguments can be derived from this conditional statement?

If a man longs for his childhood home, what he really longs for is his childhood.

1. If a man longs for his childhood home, then what he really longs for is his childhood.

This man longs for his childhood home.

So

He longs for his childhood.

Affirms the antecedent.

2. If a man longs for his childhood home, then what he really longs for is his childhood.

This man does not long for his childhood.

So

He does not long for his childhood home.

Denies the consequent.

QUIZ

1. Rewrite the following argument in standard form. Identify the conditional statement, the second reason, and conclusion.

   The food service on campus will not improve unless the students protest. The students are not going to protest, so the food service will not improve.

   Conditional statement: If the students do not protest, then the food service on campus will not improve.

   Second reason: The students are not going to protest.

   Conclusion: The food service will not improve.

2. Identify what happened in the second reason of the argument (i.e., what was affirmed or denied?).

   The antecedent was affirmed.

3. Is this argument valid or invalid? **valid**

TEST ITEMS

True or False

1. <u>T</u> F Affirming the antecedent in a conditional argument is sometimes referred to by the Latin name *modus ponens*.
2. T <u>F</u> Affirming the antecedent will, by itself, make a conditional argument reasonable. **[It only renders the argument *valid*.]**
3. <u>T</u> F Denying the consequent in a conditional argument is sometimes referred to by the Latin name *modus tollens*.
4. T <u>F</u> Conditional statements that include "only if" should be read, "If . . . then not . . . ." **["If *not* . . . then not . . . ."]**
5. <u>T</u> F "Unless" affects only the antecedent of the conditional statement.
6. T <u>F</u> A necessary condition is defined as a condition under which some other event will occur.
7. <u>T</u> F The statements, "If not B, then not A," and "A only if B," say the same thing about the relationship between A and B.
8. <u>T</u> F The slippery slope argument is a type of argument from direction.
9. <u>T</u> F The argument from direction can be thought of as a series of linked conditional arguments.

10. <u>T</u> F Invalid conditional arguments either deny the antecedent or affirm the consequent of their conditional statements.
11. <u>T</u> F Disjunctive arguments are a kind of enumeration argument.
12. <u>T</u> F In dilemma arguments, the two alternatives presented are usually both undesirable.
13. T <u>F</u> An enumeration argument must account for every conceivable alternative.
14. <u>T</u> F Valid enumeration arguments—provided the disjuncts are not exclusive—will proceed by eliminating alternatives until one or none is left.
15. <u>T</u> F In a conditional argument the wording must remain consistent throughout, or a false conclusion might be drawn from what appears to be a valid argument.
16. <u>T</u> F Two alternatives, expressed as disjuncts, that might be both true at the same time are called inclusive disjuncts.

Multiple Choice

1. These arguments set out alternative explanations or options, then follow a process of elimination.
    - <u>a.</u>   enumeration arguments
    - b.   direction arguments
    - c.   generalizations
    - d.   arguments from inconsistency
    - e.   conditional arguments

2. "If A, then B. A, therefore B" reflects the structure of
    - a.   enumeration arguments
    - b.   dilemmas
    - c.   disjunctives
    - d.   arguments from inconsistency
    - <u>e.</u>   conditional arguments

3. Two enumerated alternatives marked by an "either/or" statement.
    - a.   enumeration arguments
    - b.   dilemma
    - <u>c.</u>   disjuncts
    - d.   argument from inconsistency
    - e.   *tu quoque* argument

4. It is valid in a disjunctive argument consisting of inclusive disjuncts to
    - a.   affirm a disjunct
    - <u>b.</u>   deny a disjunct
    - c.   affirm or deny either disjunct
    - d.   accept a disjunct
    - e.   reject a disjunct

Chapter 10 Validity in Conditional and Enumeration Arguments

5. A condition without which some other event will not occur.
    <u>a.</u> a necessary condition
    b. a causal condition
    c. a categorical condition
    d. a sufficient condition
    e. a and d

6. Disjunctions that force a choice between limited and undesirable alternatives.
    a. enumeration arguments
    <u>b.</u> dilemmas
    c. conditional arguments
    d. argument from inconsistency
    e. categorical arguments

7. The "if" clause in a conditional statement.
    a. connective
    b. consequent
    c. affirmation
    <u>d.</u> antecedent
    e. denial

8. A condition that brings about another event.
    <u>a.</u> sufficient condition
    b. adequate condition
    c. affirming the consequent
    d. necessary condition
    e. conditional relationship

9. A condition without which another event will not occur.
    a. sufficient condition
    b. adequate condition
    c. affirming the consequent
    <u>d.</u> necessary condition
    e. conditional relationship

10. Placing the following conditional statement in standard form would produce which of the following statements?

    Iran will suspend its nuclear weapons program only if the United States lifts all trade sanctions.

    a. If Iran suspends its nuclear weapons program, the United States will lift all trade sanctions.
    <u>b.</u> If the United States does not lift all trade sanctions, then Iran will not suspend its nuclear weapons program.
    c. If Iran does not suspend its nuclear weapons program, then the United States will not lift all trade sanctions.
    d. If the United States lifts all trade sanctions, then Iran will suspend its nuclear weapons program.
    e. All Iranian nuclear weapons programs are cases of the United States lifting all trade sanctions.

Terminology

Provide the correct term for the following definitions.

1. The "if-then" statements in conditional arguments. **conditional statements**
2. The "if" clause in a conditional statement. **antecedent**
3. The "then" clause in a conditional statement. **consequent**
4. A condition that brings about another event. **sufficient condition**
5. A condition without which another event cannot occur. **necessary condition**
6. Sets out alternative explanations or options and then follows a process of elimination. **enumeration argument**
7. Disjunctions that force a choice between limited and undesirable options. **dilemmas**
8. An argument that strings together two or more conditional statements to predict a remote result from a first step. **argument from direction**
9. Two alternatives, expressed as disjuncts, that cannot both be true at the same time. **exclusive disjuncts**
10. A dilemma argument that employs artificially limited options to mislead an audience. **false dilemma**

Short Answer

1. What are the two ways of making a valid inference from a conditional statement?

    1. affirm the antecedent

    2. deny the consequent

2. Translate the following statement into an "if-then" statement: The paper will continue to be delivered unless you cancel it.

    If you do not cancel the paper, then it will continue to be delivered.

3. Translate the following statement into an "if-then" statement: The professor will respond only if you ask him.

    If you do not ask the professor, then he will not respond.

4. In the following statement, is A a necessary or sufficient condition for B?

    If A: the animal is a whale, then B: it is a mammal.

    sufficient condition

5. Provide another conditional statement that expresses the same relationship between A and B as the following: A only if B.

    If not B then not A.

6. What two conditions must a reasonable enumeration argument satisfy, in addition to validity?

    1. All the plausible alternatives must be enumerated.

    2. All of the alternatives that were treated as eliminated must actually be eliminated.

Chapter 10   Validity in Conditional and Enumeration Arguments

Application

Translate the following conditional arguments into a standard "if-then" form, if necessary. Test their validity, and indicate whether each is valid or invalid.

1. No major political change in this nation will come about unless the people vote. The people are beginning to vote, so we can expect to see major political change.

   If the people do not vote, then no major political change in this nation will come about.

   The people are beginning to vote,

   Conclusion: so we can expect to see major political change.

   Denies the antecedent, invalid.

2. If Anderson cooperates, then he will be given a reduced sentence. He is cooperating, so he will get a reduced sentence.

   Affirms the antecedent, valid. [Already in standard form.]

3. That animal over there is not a cat unless it sleeps all day. It does sleep all day, so it must be a cat.

   If that animal over there does not sleep all day, then it is not a cat.

   It does sleep all day,

   Conclusion: so it must be a cat.

   Invalid, denies the antecedent.

4. We should explore space only if the problems on earth are solved. The problems on earth are not solved. Thus, we should not explore space.

   If the problems on earth are not solved, then we should not explore space.

   The problems on earth are not solved.

   Conclusion: Thus, we should not explore space.

   Valid, affirms the antecedent.

5. The government can't claim success for its economic policies unless there is a steady drop in the price of consumer goods. And the government certainly can't claim the success of its economic policies, so there has not been a drop in the price of consumer goods.

   If there is not a steady drop in the price of consumer goods, then the government can't claim success for its economic policies.

   And the government certainly can't claim the success of its economic policies,

   Conclusion: so there has not been a drop in the price of consumer goods.

   Invalid, affirms the consequent.

6. Rewrite the following conditional argument in standard form. State specifically what occurs in the argument's second reason. Indicate whether the argument is valid or invalid.

You will not be in line for the promotion you want unless you finish your MBA. You will get the promotion, because you are going to finish your MBA.

Standardization:

If you do not finish your MBA, then you will not be in line for the promotion you want.

You are going to finish your MBA.

So you will get the promotion.

Denies the antecedent.

Invalid.

Identification

Identify the following arguments by type:

1. One side or the other is going to win in this conflict, regardless of whether we are pleased with either. Admittedly, both sides have shown a willingness to disregard basic human rights, but we must back the one most likely to work for our interests in the region, and that means sending aid to the rebels. **dilemma**

2. The new fighter jet crash was caused either by a problem in the engine, the on-board computers, or pilot error. Because the investigation has eliminated pilot error and the computers, we are left to conclude that the problem was with the engine. **enumeration argument**

3. The pleasure derived from smoking marijuana eventually diminishes. This leads to a desire for harder drugs that can produce that first "high." Because the same gradual diminution of effect will accompany every new drug, the search for a new high goes on and on. Eventually, "social" users of marijuana find themselves addicted to heroin or "crack." So, the best advice I can give you is not to smoke that first joint. **argument from direction**

4. Affirmative action is justified injustice. It is a tragic choice but one which has to be made because the alternative of racial discrimination is unacceptable in a civilized society. **dilemma**

Chapter 11
Validity in Categorical Arguments

EXERCISES

A. For the following categorical arguments, identify each statement as one of the four standard forms, for example, universal affirmative. Identify the middle terms and end terms in each. Using **D** and **U**, mark the distribution of each term. Applying the three rules of validity for categorical arguments, indicate whether each is valid or invalid.

             D   **U**

1. All / tour guides / are / polite /. **UA**

              D   **U**

   All / tour-bus drivers / are / polite /. **UA**

   Therefore

              D   **U**

   All / tour-bus drivers / are / tour guides /. **UA**

   Middle term: polite

   End terms: tour-bus drivers, tour guides

   The argument is invalid as the middle term is not distributed exactly once, and as the end term "tour guides" is distributed only once.

             D   **U**

2. All / New Englanders / are / explorers /. **UA**

          D   **D**

   No / explorers / are / cautious /. **UN**

   Therefore

          D   **D**

   No / New Englanders / are / cautious /. **UN**

   Middle term: explorers

   End terms: New Englanders, cautious

   The argument is valid.

3.   **D**   **U**
All / company employees / are / well trained /. **UA**

        U   **D**
Some / well-trained people / are not / competent /. **PN**

Thus

        U   **D**
Some / company employees / are not / competent /. **PN**

Middle term: well trained

End terms: company employees, competent

The argument is invalid: the middle term is not distributed exactly once; "company employees," an end term, is distributed only once.

4.   **D**   **U**
All / members of the Civic Party / are / political opportunists /. **UA**

        D   **U**
All / political opportunists / are / members of the Central Committee /. **UA**

So

        D   **U**
All / members of the Central Committee / are / members of the Civic Party /.
                                                                                              UA

Middle term: political opportunists

End terms: members of the Central Committee, members of the Civic Party

Argument is invalid as both of the end terms are distributed only once.

5.   **D**   **U**
All / poems by Poe / are / poems that use iambic pentameter /. **UA**

        D   **D**
No / poems in this collection / are / poems that use iambic pentameter /. **UN**

Thus,

        D   **D**
No / poems in this collection / are / poems by Poe /. **UN**

Middle term: poems using iambic pentameter

End terms: poems in this collection, poems by Poe

The argument is valid.

Chapter 11 Validity in Categorical Arguments

B. Put the following arguments into standard form and mark the distribution of terms. Find the missing statement by applying the rules of validity.

1. None of the men who rented the car were bald, though some men who rented the truck were bald.

         D   **D**
No / men who rented the car / are / bald [men] /. **UN**

         U   **U**
Some / men who rented the truck / were / bald [men] /. **PA**

Thus,

         U   **D**
Some / men who rented the truck / are not / men who rented the car /. **PN**
                                                       [missing conclusion]

2. Several members of the bargaining team are retired teachers, though all members of the bargaining team are members of the teachers' union.

         U   **U**
Some / members of the bargaining team / are / retired teachers /. **PA**

         D   **U**
All / members of the bargaining team / are / members of the teachers' union /.
                                                                       UA

         U   **U**
Some / retired teachers / are / members of the teachers' union /. **PA**
                                                       [missing conclusion]

3. The actors in that play could not have been graduates of the theatre program, because none of them came to the defense of the director.

         D   **D**
No / actors in that play / are / people who came to the defense of the director /.
                                                                       UN

         D   **U**
All / graduates of the theatre program / are / people who came to the defense
                                                        of the director /. **UA [missing reason]**

Thus

         D   **D**
No / actors in that play / are / graduates of the theatre program /. **UN**

Part IV Validity: The Structure of Arguments

4. All the papers in the Twain Collection belong to the Twain estate, and all the items belonging to the Twain estate are currently being sold at auction.

                D   U

All / papers in the Twain Collection / are / items belonging to the Twain estate /. **UA**

                D   U

All / items belonging to the Twain estate / are / items currently being sold at auction /. **UA**

Thus

                D   U

All / papers in the Twain Collection / are currently being sold at auction /. **UA**

                                                                               [missing conclusion]

5. All forms of cruel and unusual punishment are prohibited by the Constitution. All cases of solitary confinement are forms of cruel and unusual punishment.

              D   U

All / forms of cruel and unusual punishment / are / prohibited by the Constitution /. **UA**

              D   U

All / cases of solitary confinement / are / forms of cruel and unusual punishment /. **UA**

Thus,

              D   U

All / cases of solitary confinement / are / prohibited by the Constitution /. **UA**

ADDITIONAL EXERCISES

A. Identify all the following statements by type. Test the arguments for validity. For each, identify the end terms and the middle term. Show the distribution of all terms in the arguments.

1.

              D   D

No / Saints / are / egotistical /. **UN**

              D   U

All / members of the New Orleans football team / are / Saints /. **UA**

              D   U

All / members of the New Orleans football team / are / egotistical /. **UA**

End terms: members of New Orleans football team, egotistical
Middle term: Saints
Invalid: End term rule broken. Negation rule broken.

2.

                U   U
Some / involuntary actions / are / helpful /. **PA**

             U   D
Some / public actions / are not / helpful /. **PN**

             U   D
Some / public actions / are not / involuntary actions /. **PN**

End terms: public actions, involuntary actions

Middle term: helpful (actions)

Invalid: End term rule broken.

B. Put the following statements into standard form. To the right of each statement, indicate which type of statement it is. Using **U** and **D**, mark the distribution of terms. Identify the end terms and the middle term. Assuming the syllogism is valid, find the missing statement by showing what the distribution of the terms in the missing statement must be.

Some members of the Green Party are not involved citizens, because some members of the Green Party do not vote.

            U   D
Some / members of the Green Party / are not / people who vote /. **PN**

     D   U
All / involved citizens / are / people who vote /. **UA**

            U   D
Some / members of the Green Party / are not / involved citizens /. **PN**

Middle term: people who vote

End terms: members of the Green Party, involved citizens

Distribution of terms in missing statement:
involved citizens: D
people who vote: U

Part IV Validity: The Structure of Arguments

C. Identify the types of statements in the following syllogism. Using **U** and **D**, show the distribution of terms. Identify the middle term and the end terms. Indicate whether any fallacies are committed, and if so, which rules are broken.

          U   **U**
Some / generals / are / egotistical /. **PA**

          D   **D**
No / colonels / are / generals /. **UA**

          U   **D**
Some / colonels / are not / egotistical. / **PN**

Middle term: generals

End terms: colonels, egotistical

Rules broken:
2. (ET) broken: Both end terms are unequally distributed.

TEST ITEMS

True or False

1. <u>T</u> F   In a valid categorical argument, neither end term may be distributed only once.
2. T <u>F</u>   In a valid categorical argument, the middle term must be distributed twice.
3. <u>T</u> F   In a universal negative statement, both subject and predicate terms are distributed.
4. <u>T</u> F   A distributed term makes reference to every member of the category it represents.
5. <u>T</u> F   End terms connect reasons or premises to conclusions.
6. T <u>F</u>   In a universal affirmative statement there are no distributed terms.
7. <u>T</u> F   A middle term appears in both reasons of a categorical argument.
8. T <u>F</u>   Categorical arguments contain one end term and two middle terms.
9. T <u>F</u>   In a valid categorical argument, the end terms must be distributed twice.
10. <u>T</u> F   In a valid categorical argument the number of negative reasons and the number of negative conclusions must be equal.

Multiple Choice

Select the most specific completion of the statement.

1. All A are B is a
    - <u>a.</u> universal affirmative statement.
    - b. universal negative statement.
    - c. particular affirmative statement.
    - d. particular negative statement.
    - e. categorical statement.

2. Some A are not B is a
    a. universal affirmative statement.
    b. universal negative statement.
    c. particular affirmative statement.
    <u>d.</u> particular negative statement.
    e. categorical statement.

3. No A are B is a
    a. universal affirmative statement.
    <u>b.</u> universal negative statement.
    c. particular affirmative statement.
    d. particular negative statement.
    e. categorical statement.

4. Some A are B is a
    a. universal affirmative statement.
    b. universal negative statement.
    <u>c.</u> particular affirmative statement.
    d. particular negative statement.
    e. categorical statement.

5. There are no distributed terms in
    a. a universal affirmative statement.
    b. a universal negative statement.
    <u>c.</u> a particular affirmative statement.
    d. a particular negative statement.
    e. a categorical statement.

6. Only the subject term is distributed in
    <u>a.</u> a universal affirmative statement.
    b. a universal negative statement.
    c. a particular affirmative statement.
    d. a particular negative statement.
    e. a categorical statement.

7. The subject and the predicate terms are distributed in
    a. a universal affirmative statement.
    <u>b.</u> a universal negative statement.
    c. a particular affirmative statement.
    d. a particular negative statement.
    e. a categorical statement.

8. Only the predicate term is distributed in
    a. a universal affirmative statement.
    b. a universal negative statement.
    c. a particular affirmative statement.
    <u>d.</u> a particular negative statement.
    e. a categorical statement.

Short Answer

1. A statement claiming that all members of one group are also members of some other group. **universal affirmative statement**

2. Provide the three rules of validity for categorical arguments.

    1. The middle term must be distributed exactly once.

    2. Neither end term may be distributed only once.

    3. The number of negative premises must equal the number of negative conclusions.

3. A categorical statement that asserts that some members of one group are also members of another group. **particular affirmative**

4. A name for any categorical statement in which the subject and predicate terms are distributed similarly. **convertible statement**

5. A categorical statement claiming that some members of one group are not members of another group. **particular negative**

Application

Rewrite the following arguments in standard form. Show the distribution of terms (using **D** and **U**), and apply the appropriate tests to the following categorical syllogisms. State which of the rules of validity are broken by each argument. If the argument breaks no rule, label it valid.

1. Some art courses are valuable courses to take, and some valuable courses are not expensive. So, no art courses are expensive ones.

               U   U
    Some / art courses / are / valuable courses to take /.

                 U   D
    Some / valuable courses / are not / expensive /.

           D   D
    No / art courses / are / expensive courses /.

    The middle term—valuable courses—is not distributed, and thus the argument breaks the first rule. The end term, art courses, is distributed only once. It thus breaks the second rule.

2. Some professors are creative, since all creative people show sensitivity and all professors exhibit sensitivity.

             D   U
    All / creative people / are / sensitive /.

           D   U
    All / professors / are / sensitive /.

            U   U
    Some / professors / are / creative /.

    The middle term—sensitive—is not distributed at all. It breaks the first rule. The end terms—professors and creative people—are both distributed only once, and thus break rule two.

3. Find the missing statement (either a reason or a conclusion) that would complete the following categorical argument and make it valid. Identify the statements by type (for example, particular affirmative). Mark the distribution of all terms using **D** and **U** in all three statements. Identify the middle term (**MT**) and end terms (**ET**).

Some aquatic animals are not reptiles, because some aquatic animals are not cold-blooded.

      U   D
Some / aquatic animals / are not / cold-blooded /. **PN**

        D   U
[missing reason] All / reptiles / are / cold-blooded /. **UA**

      U   D
Some / aquatic animals / are not / reptiles /. **PN**

ET: aquatic animals, reptiles

MT: cold-blooded

PART V
Linguistic Consistency: Language in Argument

Chapter 12
Definition in Argument

EXERCISES

A. Identify the strategies of definition—euphemism, reclassificaton, or labeling—employed in the following.

1. The suggestion that the new CD by Slash and Trash should be banned from record stores amounts to censorship. Moreover, the critics misunderstand the musical intent of these sincere, sensitive young artists.

The act of banning a CD is defined strategically—labeled—as "censorship" in order to allow a condemnation of the act. The musicians are also defined into the category "artists" in order to secure protection of their lyrics—a second instance of labeling.

2. Why shouldn't college athletes be paid, and paid well? After all, they are primarily entertainers, and entertainers are paid well.

Here, college athletes are reclassified as "entertainers," thus allowing the conclusion regarding pay.

3. A fetus cannot think, choose, or envision a future. Thus, a fetus is potentially a person but not a full person. As merely a potential person, a fetus does not have the rights of a full person.

The fetus is defined as "potentially a person," which is distinguished here from "a full person." Again, conclusions follow from this instance of reclassification.

4. An advertisement reads: Metrofund debt solutions—it's not a loan, it's a way out of debt.

The term "loan" is simply redefined as a "way out of debt." This is a euphemism.

5. Techniques such as sleep deprivation and exposure to extreme heat or cold are not torture, but aggressive interrogation techniques.

"Aggressive interrogation techniques" is offered as a euphemism.

6. The president avoided the use of the term "mistake," preferring instead to call his errors in judgment "miscalculations."

"Miscalculations" is substituted for "mistake." This change renders the president's "errors in judgment" less serious matters.

7. Sugar is a type of poison, which is clear when we see its effects on the health of children and adults.

Sugar is labeled "poison" in this example.

8. My client did leak classified material to WikiLeaks, but this does not make him a traitor. He is a whistle-blower.

The client is reclassified in this example, moved from the category of "traitor" to the category of "whistle-blower." Some students may want to call this an example of euphemism, which it may be, depending upon one's political leanings. Apparently the attorney involved in making this argument is seeking a *more* accurate classification of the client.

B. Identify the source of definition suggested in the following examples. Provide a possible response to each that might appeal to a different source of definition, or that questions how the definition is interpreted.

1. I opposed amnesty for war criminals, as the word amnesty comes from the Latin word *amnestia*, which means to forget. We should never forget the terrible things that were done in the region.

The source of definition is etymology. A response might be that the term is being used according to common usage—to not prosecute—and not according to etymology.

2. State law governing public education defines bullying as aggressive and unwanted behavior directed by one student at another, where there also exists a power imbalance such as age, size, or social status. The case before us is not a case of bullying, because the alleged victim is bigger than the alleged bully.

Authority is the source of definition for "bullying." A narrow definition of power from the standpoint of common understanding also plays a part here. A response to the argument might be that power imbalance might still be present in age or social status.

3. Everybody knows that marriage is a public bond between a man and a woman, so same-sex marriage violates even common sense understanding of marriage.

The appeal here is to common usage, but the assertion that "everybody knows" is an exaggeration. The definition of marriage in common usage is shifting.

4. The best way to understand great art is to experience it directly. When you are listening to a Beethoven symphony or looking at a painting by Rembrandt, you know you are in the presence of great art.

Here the definition of "great art" is from paradigm case. A response might involve pointing out that other paradigm cases of great art could be advanced that would broaden the category. Another tack would involve defining "great art" by common usage or authority.

5. The founders of this club defined "a member in good standing" as a "gentleman of good standing in the community who has paid his dues and who adheres to the values set out in the club's constitution." The terms "gentleman" and "his" make it clear that they had a male-only membership in mind. Thus, the club's bylaws restrict membership to men.

The definition of a "member in good standing" is derived from the original intent of the founders. It could be pointed out that the masculine language of the founders may have followed common usage of their day, while a more contemporary definition of a member might involve more inclusive language.

C. Which specific approach to evaluating definitions is being employed in this example? Explain your answer.

> We are being urged to buy US-made cars to help revive the economy, but what does "US-made" mean when we are talking about cars? Is Ford a US-made car? The Ford Fusion is built in Mexico. How about Chevrolet? The Chevrolet Camaro and Impala are made in Canada. On the other hand, the Honda Accord and Toyota Camry are assembled here in the United States. It can be very difficult to make the distinction between US and foreign.

Distinction without a difference is being challenged, as is clear from the last line. The individual making this argument is asserting that any distinction between US-made and foreign, when applied to automobiles, is a meaningless distinction, one based on no real differences.

D. Identify the places in the following example where argumentative definition and definition report are used.

> Despite assurances from Google about free access to digital books, Google Search represents a monopoly on orphaned books—books that are out of print but still under copyright. Google will effectively own the rights to all such books.

"Orphaned books" receives a definition report. Google's goal of digitizing all orphaned books is being defined argumentatively as a monopoly. The act of digitizing orphaned books does not fit the standard definition of a monopoly—the control of an entire industry intended to prevent competition and drive up prices. No one saw any potential profit in orphaned books before Google began this project, and such books certainly did not represent an industry. Moreover, it is not clear that Google would have exclusive rights to digitize these books. Thus, again, this is not an example of a monopoly.

QUIZ

1. Provide the term for the following definitions:

   a. Controversial definition employed in argument to categorize an object or act so as to support a certain conclusion. **argumentative definition**

   b. A less objectionable and often less accurate term exchanged for a harsh, condemning, or emotionally charged term. **euphemism**

2. What source of definition is appealed to in the following two examples?

   a. If we wish to understand the term "parent" accurately, we must return to its origins in the Latin term *parere*, which means to bear offspring. **etymology**

   b. A law student consults a legal dictionary for a definition of "tort." **authority**

TEST ITEMS

True or False

1. T **F**   To define a term by authority is to advance a representative case of the thing in question.
2. T **F**   To define a term by reference to a paradigm case is to look at the word's origins.
3. **T** F   Reclassification is a strategy of definition whereby a case or proposal is placed under a new heading to facilitate defense or accusation.
4. **T** F   Argumentative definition and categorical reasoning are very closely related.
5. **T** F   Context is very important to determining which definition is appropriate to resolving a particular issue.
6. **T** F   A law dictionary is one example of an authority that might be employed as a source of definition.
7. **T** F   A definition report is a definition that all parties to a debate agree upon, and that states a generally accepted or agreed upon meaning.
8. **T** F   Definitions establish categories into which a person, an idea, or an action is placed.
9. T **F**   Argumentative definitions are widely accepted, and thus do not advance criteria that reflect values, beliefs, and assumptions.
10. **T** F   A euphemism is a less objectionable and often less accurate term exchanged for a harsh or emotionally charged term.

Multiple Choice

1. Defining by considering the origin of a word.
    - a. common usage
    - **b.** etymology
    - c. authority
    - d. paradigm case
    - e. intent

2. Less objectionable and often less accurate terms exchanged for harsh, condemning, or emotionally charged terms.
    - a. syllogisms
    - b. enthymemes
    - **c.** euphemisms
    - d. ambiguity
    - e. equivocations

3. Defining by using a representative example of the object in question.
    a. common usage
    <u>b.</u> paradigm case
    c. authority
    d. etymology
    e. original intent

4. Defining by referring to what the initial definer of a term meant by it.
    a. common usage
    b. paradigm case
    c. authority
    d. etymology
    <u>e.</u> original intent

5. Placing a case or proposal under a new heading to facilitate defense or accusation.
    <u>a.</u> reclassification
    b. ambiguity
    c. equivocation
    d. original intent
    e. etymology

6. Defining a term only by reference to factors inherent to the claim in which it is employed.
    a. reclassification
    b. ambiguity
    c. equivocation
    d. original intent
    <u>e.</u> circular definition

7. A definition that suggests that a category exists, without explaining how objects in this category differ from those in similar categories.
    a. labeling
    b. reclassification
    c. circular definition
    d. euphemism
    <u>e.</u> distinction without a difference

8. Condemning or commending a person, group, idea, or institution by use of a suggestive name or term rather than through presenting reasons.
    <u>a.</u> labeling
    b. reclassification
    c. circular definition
    d. euphemism
    e. distinction without a difference

Terminology

1. Controversial definition employed in an argument to categorize an object or act so as to support a certain conclusion. **argumentative definition**

2. Less objectionable and often less accurate term exchanged for harsh, condemning, or emotionally charged term. **euphemism**

3. Placing a case or proposal under a new heading to facilitate defense or accusation. **reclassification**

4. Defining a term only by reference to factors inherent to the claim in which it is employed. **circular definition**

5. A source of definition that refers to a word's origins. **etymology**

6. To define a term by reference to a representative example of the term or category in question. **paradigm case**

Short Answer

1. Provide two tests that might be used to evaluate a definition.

    1. Is the definition standard or generally accepted?

    2. Did the definition originate with an appropriate source?

2. Identify four sources of definition.

    common usage, etymology, paradigm case, intent, authority

Chapter 13
Ambiguity, Equivocation, and Other Language Considerations

EXERCISES

A. For the following examples, identify the term or phrase that is ambiguous. What are the possible meanings in each case?

1. I walked all the way across campus to hear the bacteria talk.

"Bacteria talk" can mean either "to hear some bacteria conversing," or "to hear a lecture on bacteria."

2. Marine Corps Stamps Out Wednesday.

"Stamps out" can mean either "eliminates" or "postage stamps are being issued." Students will usually add "marches out" as a third alternative.

3. Perplexed by the disappearance of his sister, Vincent stood at the edge of the lake and thought, "Phyllis is at the bottom of this!"

"At the bottom of this"—of the disappearance, or of the lake. This ambiguity creates another: is Phyllis his sister, or a suspect in his sister's disappearance?

4. Woman Decapitated in Freak Accident before Attending Lecture.

"Before attending"—either she did not attend (likely) or did attend (headless) after the accident.

5. Famous culinary columnist advises cooking party guests.

"Cooking party guests"—"cooking" is either a verb or an adjective, the latter being intended.

6. Princeton Freshman wants QB Shot.

"QB shot"—wants an opportunity to play QB, or wants the current QB assassinated.

7. Scientists to Count Kangaroo Rats from Outer Space.

"From Outer Space"—can indicate the location of the count itself (i.e., the count is to be done using a satellite) or the origin of the kangaroo Rats (as in, They Came from Outer Space).

8. Free Pony Rides Threatened Here.

"Threatened" is the problem term—are free pony rides being brought to the area, or taken away? One student suggested that "Free Pony" might be a Native American, and "Threatened" his horse.

9. The shady dealings at the fertilizer factory finally got to Hal. "This whole business stinks," he said.

"Business" can refer to either the fertilizer business or to the shady dealings mentioned. "Stinks" is also ambiguous because it can mean either "smells bad" or "is morally suspect."

10. Campus police were requested to kick the fraternity members off the roof of the library.

"Kick them off" could mean "make them leave," or literally "propel them from the roof with a swift foot."

B. Identify the equivocal term in each of the following examples. Provide in your own words the two different meanings the equivocal word conveys.

1. Some people say that homosexuality is acceptable because it is natural to some individuals. However, I don't find that homosexual behavior is exhibited in nature, that is, in other animals. So how can people say it's natural?

"Natural" is equivocal. It can mean
1. an unchosen or innate inclination
or
2. occurring commonly in nature

2. The Marines have a new recruiting slogan, "A commitment to something greater than themselves." I just don't agree. There is nothing of greater value than the individual human being.

The equivocal phrase "greater than themselves" may mean
1. of more value than the individual
or
2. larger, more powerful, or of vaster scope than the individual

3. You said the movie was good because the critics liked it. But it's obvious that it wasn't any good, because the studio lost money on it.

"Good" can mean
1. expressing artistic qualities
or
2. profitable

4. I read a study that claimed that chimpanzees are more evolved than human beings, but I don't see how this can be. After all, if chimps were more evolved than we are, wouldn't they be doing these studies on us?

The phrase "more evolved" is equivocal. In the first use it means that chimpanzees have gone through more evolutionary changes than have humans. In the second use it means something like "more advanced" or "more intelligent."

Chapter 13 Ambiguity, Equivocation, and Other Language Considerations

5. Persons have rights, including the right to free speech. The Supreme Court has ruled that corporations are persons, so corporations have constitutionally protected rights just like all citizens of this country do.

The term "person" is equivocal. In the first instance it means "an individual human being with the rights of a citizen." In the second use it means that the Supreme Court has ruled that corporations are treated as persons in the sense that they have a right to exercise free speech in the form of campaign contributions. The second use of "person" is more limited that the first use, which suggests a wider range of rights for the individual citizen.

C. Explain the response to an equivocal term that is being advanced in this example.

What does socialized medicine mean? "Socialized" carries with it a negative connotation for many people in the United States, and yet can mean simply that the government is involved with the financial backing of medical care. The term can also mean a particular political philosophy which opposes private ownership and sees a central government as responsible for the entire economy. By exploiting this double meaning, the opponents of government-backed medical care can make it appear to be associated with communism or Marxism.

The response being offered is to reveal the equivocation by identifying two distinct meanings for the term in question.

D. Identify the specific problem of language reflected in each of the following statements.

1. This class is suitable for beginning through advanced levels and everyone in between.

redundancy: "beginning through advanced" includes the idea of "everyone in between."

2. I have investigated the topic from one end of the political pole to the other.

wrong word: "spectrum," not "pole," which *is* an end.

3. Leaders on both sides refuse to work for compromise, hoping instead for the inhalation of their enemies.

wrong word: "annihilation," not "inhalation"

4. The changes proposed for bringing more fans to baseball games just don't cut the bill.

misuse of a common expression—the expression is "fit the bill." It has apparently been combined with "cut the mustard."

5. He self-taught himself everything there was to know about navigation.

redundancy. The statement should read "He is self-taught . . . ." or "He taught himself . . . ."

E. Each of the following sentences reflects a problem with one or more words. Which word or words cause the problem? Which word or words should have been used?

1. The biblical profits **[prophets]** spoke the message in their own words.

2. He advanced a good argument, one that most people should easily except **[accept]**.

3. With the acception **[exception]** of only two books, all his novels are about women.

4. It was the mourning **[morning]** before the big state track meet, and our coach decided it was a good time to give us a pep talk.

5. The audience was made up entirely of perspective **[prospective]** student athletes.

6. Based on her critical reading of this historical novel, she accused the author of being anti-semantic **[anti-Semitic]**.

7. During the ceremony to commemorate the five hundredth anniversary of Columbus's voyage, one of his ancestors **[descendants]** gave a very memorable speech.

8. I chose to discuss weather **[whether]** the NEA should be abolished.

9. My uncle was involved in a very serious accident in which his foot was decapitated [**severed**]. ["Decapitated" refers to losing one's head]

10. Justice can become a very ridged **[rigid]** concept in some courtrooms.

11. An excellent example of when the death penalty should have been utilized is that of cereal **[serial]** killers.

12. I will try to explain how I derive **[arrive]** at the conclusion that more gun control laws will not help control violence.

13. This passage eludes **[alludes]** to the tremendous power of ancient Rome.

14. Lewis had a sorted **[sordid]** past.

15. Companies are now reluctant to higher **[hire]** executives who lack graduate degrees.

16. I believe that the Bible can be used to guide our lives, as long as we interrupt **[interpret]** the text in the right way.

17. Even when prisoners guilty of serious crimes such as murder are incarcerated for life, there are still possibilities such as escape, early release, and payroll **[parole]**.

18. Exact statistics on the number of homeless people in the United States very **[vary]** greatly.

19. Though it isn't a perfect solution, this new bill is defiantly **[definitely]** a step in the right direction.

20. The new rules state that a doctor is not aloud **[allowed]** to discuss his or her employment status with a patient.

Chapter 13 Ambiguity, Equivocation, and Other Language Considerations

F. The following sentences have errors in grammar, punctuation, or structure. Suggest how each sentence might be rewritten for greater clarity.

1. Cost overruns, which have become common in building nuclear power plants, have made this source of energy far less economical than was previously thought at its onset.

Cost overruns have become common in building nuclear power plants, rendering this source of energy far less economical than was previously thought.

2. I wish to show how the *Webster* decision is not only morally but constitutionally correct, and overall is what the people of the United States are pushing for and have wanted for a long time.

I wish to show how the *Webster* decision is not only morally but constitutionally correct. I will also demonstrate that the decision is what the people of the United States want.

3. Television, with its preponderance of sound bites, has become the means by which many, perhaps, sadly obtain the bulk of their information.

Television, with its preponderance of sound bites, has, perhaps sadly, become the means by which many obtain the bulk of their information.

4. The reaction was caused. By combining the two chemicals.

The reaction was caused by combining the two chemicals.

5. Values also were important because most of the athletes and their parents were looking for a school that values school first, then athletics, and I needed to express that in my speech that it is like that at my college.

Values were also important, as most of the athletes and their parents were looking for a school that emphasized academics over athletics. I needed to express in my speech that my college places such a priority on academic studies.

ADDITIONAL EXERCISES

The following statements are derived from signs intended for US tourists in other countries. Rewrite each statement to suggest what apparently was meant.

1. In an elevator in Paris: "Please leave your values **[valuables]** at the front desk."

2. On a Moscow hotel room door: "If this is your first visit to Moscow, you are welcome to it."

If this is your first visit to Moscow, we welcome you.

3. A ticket office in Copenhagen: "We take your bags and send them in all directions **[anywhere]**."

4. A hotel restaurant in Acapulco: "The manager has personally passed **[approved]** all the water served here."

5. A laundry in Rome: "Please leave your clothes **[laundry]** here and spend the day having a good time."

6. A zoo in Budapest: "Please do not feed the animals. If you have any suitable food, give it to the guard on duty."

Please do not feed the animals. If you brought food for the animals, leave it with the guard on duty.

7. Hotel across from Russian Orthodox cemetery in Moscow: "You are welcome to visit the cemetery where famous Russian composers, writers, and artists are buried daily except Thursday."

Famous Russian composers, writers, and artists are buried in this cemetery. You are welcome to visit every day except Thursday.

TEST ITEMS

True or False

1. T <u>F</u> Equivocation is substituting a less objectionable term for a harsh or offensive one.
2. <u>T</u> F When an argument contains an ambiguous term, it cannot satisfy the criterion of linguistic consistency.
3. <u>T</u> F "I know it sounds like an old touché, but the cream always rises to the top," is an example of choosing the wrong word.
4. T <u>F</u> "We're in danger of developing wrong misconceptions about this," is an example of equivocation.
5. T <u>F</u> Ambiguity and equivocation are both problems with validity.
6. <u>T</u> F When a key term is equivocal in an argument, the argument cannot satisfy the criterion of linguistic consistency.
7. T <u>F</u> Redundancy refers to a term that is not clearly defined.
8. <u>T</u> F Mixed metaphor refers to a combination of images that do not belong together.

Multiple Choice

1. More than one meaning of a word or phrase in a single context.
    a. syllogism
    b. enthymeme
    c. euphemism
    <u>d.</u> ambiguity
    e. equivocation

2. A key term changing meaning in the course of an argument.
    a. syllogism
    b. enthymeme
    c. euphemism
    d. ambiguity
    <u>e.</u> equivocation

Chapter 13 Ambiguity, Equivocation, and Other Language Considerations

3. Unnecessary repetition of an idea or term.
    <u>a.</u> redundancy
    b. mixed metaphor
    c. choosing the wrong word
    d. ambiguity
    e. equivocation

4. A combination of images that do not belong together.
    a. redundancy
    <u>b.</u> mixed metaphor
    c. choosing the wrong word
    d. ambiguity
    e. equivocation

5. Changing the meaning of a key term in the course of an argument.
    a. redundancy
    b. mixed metaphor
    c. choosing the wrong word
    d. ambiguity
    <u>e.</u> equivocation

6. More than one meaning of a key term in a single context.
    a. redundancy
    b. mixed metaphor
    c. choosing the wrong word
    <u>d.</u> ambiguity
    e. equivocation

Short Answer

1. How has the head of the Fish Advisory Board interpreted the FDA's claim in the following example? What possible problem with ambiguity is presented in this example?

    The FDA reported that eating fish may be hazardous because fish is the only flesh food that is not subject to inspection. The head of the Fish Advisory Board replied: "The idea that beef and pork are better for you because they are inspected is simply ludicrous."

    The Fish Advisory Head is taking "hazardous" to mean "unhealthful" in a nutritional sense. It clearly wasn't intended in this way, but was meant to express some danger of bacterial or chemical contamination.

Terminology

1. Repeating an idea unnecessarily. **redundancy**
2. An error in writing in which words or phrases introduce different images, thus creating a clash of ideas. **mixed metaphor**
3. More than one meaning of a word or phrase in a single context. **ambiguity**

4. A key term changing meaning in the course of an argument. **equivocation**

5. The requirement that all key terms in an argument maintain the same clear, unchanging definition throughout the argument. **linguistic consistency**

Application

A. Identify and clarify the equivocation in the following arguments:

1. You say that faith in God can be logical. However, you can't show me a logical proof for belief in God, so faith must not be reasonable.

"Logical" in this first sentence may have been intended to mean something like "reasonable." However, in the second sentence the term is taken to mean something more like "demonstrable."

2. Susan said Fred passed the bar, but he's never willing to do that when I go out with him.

"Bar": legal exam, drinking establishment

3. You said only to eat natural foods, and I am. Ice cream, potato chips, and beer are all natural foods.

"Natural" means "wholesome" in the first instance; in the second, it simply means "coming from nature."

4. I don't see why we should listen to the superintendent on the textbook issue. We need to hear from an authority in the field, and she doesn't have enough authority to get the teachers and students to do what she asks them to do.

"Authority" in the first instance means expertise; in the second instance, it means influence or control.

B. Explain which term in each of the following sentences is ambiguous. Identify the two meanings it might have.

1. Scientists discover rats in laboratories smell.

"Smell" means either "have a sense of smell," or "stink."

2. Pizzas delivered free.

"Delivered free" might mean either that the pizzas are themselves free, or that the delivery of the pizzas is without cost.

3. Local school needs to be aired.

"Aired" may mean either "discussed" or "aired out."

4. She judged from the man's dress that he was Finnish.

"Dress" refers either to a particular article of clothing—a dress—or to a manner of dressing.

5. A top executive of the firm made the tender offer, which was refused.

"Tender": "monetary" or "romantic"

6. A professor reported to the university's president that the students were revolting.

"Revolting": "disgusting" or "rebelling"

Chapter 13 Ambiguity, Equivocation, and Other Language Considerations

C. Identify a problem with language or definition in each of the following statements. Suggest a reformulation that avoids the problem.

1. A news reporter sums up a report by saying, "And so, the winds of Washington are blowing again over another political hot potato today."

mixing metaphors: the blowing wind and the hot potato apparently belong to two different figures of speech.

2. The very thought of it sent curdles up my spine.

misusing common expression: should be "sent chills up my spine." Can also be treated as choosing the wrong word—curdles rather than chills.

3. He's getting a lot of hot water over his decision.

misusing two expressions: "getting a lot of heat" and "getting into a lot of hot water."

4. Oh, it's right on the tip of my head!

misusing two expressions: "Tip of my tongue" was probably intended. Ideas are sometimes said to come "off the top of my head."

5. He was pulling in money hand over foot.

misusing common expression: "hand over fist."

6. On the third side of the coin . . . .

misusing common expression: coins have only two sides.

7. She prefers diet free drinks.

choosing the wrong word: should be either "diet drinks" or "sugar-free drinks."

8. This new faith has gone to the four corners of the globe.

misusing a common expression or choosing the wrong word: Globes don't have corners. "Ends of the earth," or perhaps "four corners of the world" would be better.

PART VI
Types and Tests of Arguments

Chapter 14
Analogies, Examples, Metonymy, and Narratives

EXERCISES

A. State which type of analogy is developed in each of the following examples—simple, judicial or *a fortiori*—along with the reasons for your identification. Identify the evidence case, conclusion case, and conclusion for each argument. Employing the tests of literal analogies, note any weaknesses that may be present in these comparisons.

1. New evidence shows that tanning beds are as carcinogenic as arsenic and cigarettes.

Evidence cases: arsenic, cigarettes

Conclusion case: tanning beds

Conclusion: Tanning beds are as carcinogenic as arsenic and cigarettes.

Type: simple literal analogy

Reason for identification: Nothing beyond a comparison of relative risks.

2. When the first heart transplant was performed in the 1960s, there were loud protests from people who claimed that such a procedure was immoral. But everyone eventually got used to the idea and forgot the moral objections entirely. The same thing will happen when people see the practical results of cloning.

Evidence case: the first heart transplant

Conclusion case: cloning

Conclusion: The same thing will happen when people see the practical results of cloning.

Type: simple literal analogy

Reason for identification: A simple comparison of cases with no additional qualities.

3. Leaders of industries that destroy the environment by their careless attitude toward pollution should be prosecuted for murder. They are murdering the earth just as surely as a killer murders a human victim.

Evidence case: a killer

Conclusion case: leaders of industries that destroy the environment

Conclusion: Leaders of industries that destroy the environment should be prosecuted for murder.

Type: judicial analogy

Reason for identification: A call for justice—"they are murdering the earth just as surely as a killer murders a human victim." Key phrase is "should be prosecuted."

4. Early humans did not exercise because their lives involved so much physical activity. That's why it's ridiculous to imagine a cave dweller going out for a jog. However, as our lives came to involve much less physical activity, exercise in the modern sense was invented. A little concentrated physical activity—running, swimming, lifting weights—was all we needed to stay healthy. Today, when our digital lives require less emotional involvement with others, it may be necessary to find ways to get just enough emotional exercise to stay psychologically healthy—like talking for a few minutes each day with a computer or a robot.

Evidence case: Early humans and physical activity

Conclusion case: Humans today and emotional activity

Conclusion: Today it may be necessary to find ways of getting just enough emotional exercise to stay psychologically healthy.

Type: Simple literal analogy

Reason for identification: direct comparison of early humans and today's humans

5. High school principal to press: "I will not allow known gang members to come to school. The threat to my students is even greater than if a child came to school with measles. If a student is involved in a gang, I will simply say, 'You stay away from the school. You are considered a threat.'"

Evidence case: students with measles

Conclusion case: student members of gangs

Conclusion: Gang members should not be allowed to come to school.

Type: *a fortiori* **analogy**

Reason for identification: The principal sees both instances as students endangering other students. The rationale for a policy procedure, not for fair treatment, is being articulated. This example might be read as a judicial analogy, though the argument is *not* advancing a plea for fair or equal treatment of the two groups. It is only arguing for student safety. Gang members are *more* dangerous than sick students, thus an *a fortiori* comparison.

6. Men and women perform the same duties in other military settings, so allowing women in combat is only fair.

Evidence case: Men in military settings

Conclusion case: Women in military settings

Conclusion: Allowing women in combat is only fair.

Type: Judicial Analogy

7. Thousands of people in the US struggle to locate adequate childcare. The government refuses to get involved, arguing that the system should remain privatized. Yet, Scandinavian countries have had nationalized childcare services since the 1970s without major problems arising and with adequate childcare available to everyone who wants it.

Evidence case: Scandinavian countries with nationalized childcare services

Conclusion case: People in US struggling to locate adequate childcare and a government that refuses to get involved

Conclusion: The US government should help families by providing nationalized childcare. (implied)

Type: simple literal analogy

Reason for identification: Though it sounds as if justice is a concern here, the argument only addresses a need, urges a solution, and notes the absence of problems in the evidence case.

8. Some people are so dense as to question whether animals really experience pain under the rigors of experimentation. Wouldn't you experience pain if those experiments were performed on you?

Evidence case: human beings (implied)

Conclusion case: animals

Conclusion: Animals feel pain during experimentation.

Type: simple literal analogy

Reason for identification: This is a simple comparison that argues that animals feel pain just as humans would under similar circumstances. Any suggestion of a policy change to bring about just treatment would be part of a subsequent line of argument.

9. You're asking whether we would be able to control the use of drugs if they were legalized. We can't even control the use of alcohol. How in the world are we supposed to be able to control the use of legalized drugs?

Evidence case: alcohol use

Conclusion case: drug use

Conclusion: How in the world are we supposed to be able to control the use of legalized drugs? [Implied: We certainly will not be able to control the use of legalized drugs.]

Type: *a fortiori* argument or super analogy

Reason for identification: Alcohol has been regulated for a long time; its regulation is carefully monitored; it is culturally familiar; and even with these factors in place, we are still unable to regulate it. Drugs pose a *more difficult* regulation problem.

10. Business writer Rich Karlgaard notes, "One-third of Los Angeles residents now tell pollsters that they are sick of their city." Karlgaard attributes much of this unhappiness to the problems associated with illegal immigration. "What religion is to contemporary U.S. national politics—a bitter and hardening divide—illegal immigration is to California politics." [Rich Karlgaard, "California Leavin'," *Forbes*, May 23, 2005, 39.]

Evidence case: religion in contemporary US national politics

Conclusion case: illegal immigration in California politics

Conclusion: Illegal immigration is a bitter and hardening divide in California politics.

Type: simple literal analogy

Reason for identification: Simple comparison of two divisive issues.

B. Identify the example or examples advanced as evidence in each of the following arguments. What general conclusion is derived from each example? Employing the tests of example arguments, identify any potential weaknesses in the examples.

1. You can buy an Aston Martin Cygnet for around $40,000. Just be aware that you are not buying an Aston Martin at all, but a Toyota iQ. Sold as a Toyota product, the same car sells for around $20,000. This is not a rare occurrence, as car companies often change the identity of a less expensive car and then double or triple the price.

Example: Same car sold as Aston Martin and Toyota

General conclusion: Car companies often change the identity of a less expensive car and then raise the price.

2. The oldest known use of zero as a placeholder in a numerical system is in Cambodia. A clear use of zero was discovered in a temple inscription dating from around 600 CE. Thus, the ancient residents of Southeast Asia had highly developed mathematical systems long before Europeans, who did not use zero until about 1100.

Example: Earliest use of zero as placeholder in Cambodia

General conclusion: Residents of Southeast Asia had highly developed mathematical systems long before Europeans.

3. Michael Jackson's life, with its many triumphs and tragedies, reveals that the US celebrity machine gives and takes away, creates heroes and saints in an instant, and just as quickly transforms them into cowards or villains.

Example: Michael Jackson's life

General conclusion: The US celebrity machine gives and takes away, creates heroes and saints in an instant, and just as quickly transforms them into cowards or villains.

4. Sea captains can be trained to be conscientious about pollution. Korea already requires all captains to be educated in the international laws governing dumping waste into the oceans. That requirement has made a major difference in the pollution-related activities of Korean ships.

Example: Korea, which requires all captains to be educated in the international laws governing dumping waste into the oceans.

Conclusion: It is possible to train sea captains to be conscientious about pollution.

5. California's new hands-free phone law shows that legislation banning hand-held cell phone use while driving can be highly effective.

Example: California's new hands-free law

General conclusion: Legislation banning hand-held cell phone use while driving can be highly effective.

C. Differentiate the following example and analogy arguments. For the analogies, identify the evidence and conclusion cases. For the example arguments, identify the example itself and the general conclusion.

1. Israel and Sweden have long accepted gay men and women into their military service and have had few, if any, security problems as a result. Thus, gay men and women should not be viewed as a security risk in military organizations.

Example argument

Examples: Israel and Sweden

General conclusion: Gay men and women should not be viewed as a security risk in military organizations.

2. An earthquake will hit San Francisco in the near future. Geologic activity around the city is similar to that around Los Angeles before the big 1971 quake. We also see changes in the ocean and atmosphere in San Francisco that are very close to changes noted just prior to the Los Angeles quake.

Analogy (simple literal)

Evidence case: Los Angeles

Conclusion case: San Francisco

3. Hewlett-Packard and Polaroid are companies that were started during the Great Depression. These cases suggest that times of economic hardship can also be times of great opportunity for savvy investors and entrepreneurs.

Example argument

Examples: Hewlett-Packard and Polaroid

General conclusion: Times of economic hardship can also be times of great opportunity for savvy investors and entrepreneurs.

4. Airline pilots perform a task in which a single error can spell disaster, much like physicians. Pilots, much like doctors, must acquire knowledge that is constantly changing. Pilots, however, must requalify periodically to keep their licenses. Physicians can practice indefinitely without requalifying. Surely, requiring such requalification of doctors is just as important.

Analogy (simple literal)

Evidence case: airline pilots

Conclusion case: physicians

5. The waste of technology in the apparently pointless use of such sites as YouTube may actually have a purpose—the more instances of a new technology's use, the more likely that someone will discover a beneficial application for it. Science fiction writer Carrie Doctorow calls this approach "thinking like a dandelion." He writes, "The disposition of each—or even most—of the seeds isn't the important thing, from a dandelion's point of view. The important thing is that every crack in every pavement is filled with dandelions. The dandelion doesn't want to nurse a single precious copy of itself. . . . The dandelion just wants to be sure that every single opportunity for reproduction is exploited."

Analogy

Evidence case: dandelion's apparently wasteful use of seeds

Conclusion case: apparently wasteful use of technology sites such as YouTube

6. Age differences are insignificant to the success of a marriage. Why, I know a couple in which the wife is seventy-two and the husband is nineteen, and they are perfectly happy.

Argument from example

Example: a couple in which the wife is seventy-two and the husband is nineteen

General conclusion: Age differences are insignificant to the success of a marriage.

7. The Bureau of Alcohol, Tobacco, Firearms, and Explosives conducted a sting operation in the San Francisco area aimed at slowing the illegal flow of guns into California from Nevada gun shows. The agency netted more than one thousand illegally imported guns in a single operation. This proves that gun shows in one state can dramatically increase the number of weapons available in a neighboring state, a claim that gun rights groups deny.

Example argument

Example: Bureau of Alcohol, Tobacco, Firearms, and Explosives sting operation in San Francisco that netted more than one thousand illegally imported guns

General conclusion: Gun shows in one state can dramatically increase the number of weapons available in a neighboring state.

8. According to Dr. Robert Massy of the Royal Astronomical Society, "galaxies form around black holes in the way that a pearl forms around grit." [Pallab Ghosh, "Black Hole Confirmed in Milky Way," BBC Online, December 9, 2008, http://news.bbc/co.uk/2/hi/science/nature/7774287.stm (Accessed July 22, 2009).]

Analogy

Evidence case: pearls

Conclusion case: galaxies

9. Caption on an anti-fur ad showing an animal's paw caught in a metal trap: "Get the feel of fur. Slam your hand in a car door!"

Analogy (simple literal)

Evidence case: slamming your hand in a car door

Conclusion case: animals being caught in steel traps [implied]

10. It has been proposed that the United States Navy return to the small, lightweight naval vessels of the 1980s and '90s as a cost-cutting measure, but the case of the *USS Stark,* which was completely incapacitated by two inexpensive air-to-surface missiles fired from an Iraqi fighter in 1987, demonstrated that small naval ships with lightweight hulls are highly vulnerable to inexpensive air-to-sea missiles.

Argument from example

Example: The *USS Stark,* which was completely incapacitated by two inexpensive air-to-surface missiles

General conclusion: Small naval ships with lightweight hulls are highly vulnerable to inexpensive air-to-sea missiles.

D. The following excerpts from famous speeches and essays suggest that figurative analogies have had a powerful impact in some important controversies. Identify the evidence relationship and conclusion relationship for each analogy.

1. *Context:* In February of 1860, Abraham Lincoln argued that the Democrats, his opponents, were making an utterly unreasonable claim concerning why voters should not elect a Republican to the presidency. A few months before the 1860 Republican National Convention, Lincoln visited New York, where he delivered the famous speech from which this figurative analogy is drawn. What is the picture presented in the evidence relationship? What is the exact relationship between the two people in the picture? To what groups did Lincoln compare these two people in his conclusion relationship?

> But you will not abide the election of a Republican President! In that supposed event, you say, you will destroy the Union; and then, you say, the great crime of having destroyed it will be upon us! That is cool. A highwayman holds a pistol to my ear, and mutters through his teeth, "Stand and deliver, or I shall kill you, and then you will be a murderer!" To be sure, what the robber demanded of me—my money—was my own; and I had a clear right to keep it; but it was no more my own than my vote is my own; and the threat of death to me, to extort my money, and the threat of destruction to the Union, to extort my vote, can scarcely be distinguished in principle. (Abraham Lincoln, Cooper Union Address)

Evidence relationship: highwayman / victim

Conclusion relationship: Democrats / voters

The relationship in both cases is, according to Lincoln, extortion of something belonging to the victim on the basis of an absurd threat that the eventual crime will be the victim's fault.

2. *Context:* Americans take for granted that their Constitution reflects good ideas about the governance of a democracy. When it was first proposed, however, the document elicited tremendous debate. James Madison, along with Alexander Hamilton and John Jay, argued vehemently for the Constitution in a series of pieces known collectively as *The Federalist Papers.* Madison developed a figurative analogy to urge adoption of the new Constitution that, he argued, may not be perfect but was clearly preferable to the Articles of Confederation. What two evidence relationships did he develop? What relationship is similar in each? What, then, is the conclusion relationship?

> It is a matter both of wonder and regret that those who raise so many objections against the new Constitution should never call to mind the defects of that which is to be exchanged for it. It is not necessary that the former should be perfect: it is sufficient that the latter is more imperfect. No man would refuse to give brass for silver or gold because the latter had some alloy in it. No man would refuse to quit a shattered and tottering habitation for a firm and commodious building because the latter had not a porch to it, or because some of the rooms might be a little larger or smaller, or the ceiling a little higher or lower than his fancy would have planned them. (James Madison, *Federalist Paper 38,* January 1788)

> **First evidence relationship: brass / silver or gold**
>
> **Second evidence relationship: old house / new house**
>
> **Conclusion relationship: Articles of Confederation / Constitution**
>
> **The relationship in all three cases is that one would be willing to exchange the former for the latter, even if the latter were imperfect.**

3. *Context:* Demosthenes, perhaps the greatest orator of ancient Greece, urged the Athenian Senate to fight Philip of Macedon as if they had some idea about how to fight. To make his point, Demosthenes presented the following analogy, developed around the Athenians' fondness for watching boxing matches between untrained foreign captives and trained Athenian boxers. It's no secret who usually won these bouts, and why. What evidence relationship did he develop in this argument? What is the conclusion relationship? What is the ironic twist that gives the argument its own "punch"?

> The citizens of Athens, however possessed as they are of the greatest power of all in ships, fighting men, cavalry, and monetary resources, have never to this day made a right use of any of them. The war against Philip exactly resembles the methods of an untaught foreigner in the boxing ring. If he is hit, he hugs the place, and if you hit him somewhere else, there go his hands again. He has not learnt, and is not prepared to defend himself or look to his front. So it is with the policy of Athens. If news comes of Philip in the Chersonese, an expedition there is voted; if it is Thermopylae, it is sent there. Wherever he goes, we hurry up and down at his instance, controlled by his strategy without any constructive military plan of our own, without foresight to anticipate news of what is happening or has happened. (Demosthenes, *Philippic I,* 351 BCE)

> **Evidence relationship: Athenian boxer / untrained foreigner**
>
> **Conclusion relationship: Philip / Athens**
>
> **The relationship is that the absence of a plan leads to defeat. Demosthenes' irony is striking (no pun intended), because he puts the Athenians in the place of the foreigner and Philip in the place of the Athenian boxer.**

E. Explain how metonymy is employed in the following example.

> British Prime Minister Benjamin Disraeli (1804–1881) was asked, shortly after the publication of Darwin's *On the Origin of Species,* which side of the debate over evolution he supported. Disraeli responded, "I am for the angels, and against the apes."
>
> **Disraeli used "angels" to represent the entire Judeo-Christian tradition, and "apes" to represent the entire theory of evolution. Disraeli was thus siding with those who opposed the idea of evolution.**

F. Think of a movie you have seen recently that you believe was arguing for a particular point of view. Write a brief analysis of the movie's coherence and fidelity as either contributing to or detracting from its persuasiveness. In addition, comment on the relationship between portrayal and point of view in the film.

ADDITIONAL EXERCISES

A. Identify the evidence case, the conclusion case, and the stated or implied conclusion for the following analogies. Identify the type of analogy for each.

1. Smoking one marijuana cigarette exposes the lungs to more tar than does smoking two packs of ordinary cigarettes. Thus, if you have given up smoking cigarettes for health reasons, you have even greater reason not to smoke marijuana.

Evidence case: smoking two packs of cigarettes

Conclusion case: smoking one marijuana cigarette

Type: *a fortiori* analogy

2. It is only fair that students be allowed to look up a difficult case in their textbooks when they are taking an examination. After all, physicians can consult reference works when diagnosing a difficult case.

Evidence case: physicians consulting reference works

Conclusion case: students looking up a difficult case in their textbooks

Type: judicial analogy

3. If you couldn't pay off an ordinary bank loan last year of $1,000 at 8 percent interest, what makes you think you can now pay off a credit card loan of $3,000 at 18 percent interest?

Evidence case: failure to pay ordinary bank loan of $1,000 at 8 percent interest

Conclusion case: paying off a credit card loan of $3,000 at 18 percent interest

Type: *a fortiori* analogy

4. Attorneys are paid by the case to consult with their clients, so teachers should also be paid to provide parents with advice about their children's educational problems.

Evidence case: attorneys

Conclusion case: teachers

Conclusion: Teachers should be paid to provide parents with advice about their children's educational problems.

TEST ITEMS

True or False

1. T **F** The evidence case in literal analogies is something unfamiliar or about which there is likely to be disagreement.
2. **T** F Judicial analogies urge fair or equal treatment for similar cases.
3. T **F** "The rule of justice" is another name for the connective for figurative analogies.
4. **T** F The success of judicial analogies depends on establishing the close similarity of the cases being compared.
5. **T** F One test of figurative analogies is to ask whether the relationships being compared are really similar.
6. T **F** Figurative analogies compare cases rather than relationships.
7. T **F** The *a fortiori* analogy argues for similar treatment of persons in similar circumstances.
8. **T** F The argument from example generalizes from one example or a small number of examples.
9. **T** F One test of the argument from example asks whether the example is typical of the category.
10. **T** F In a debate situation, a figurative analogy can often be altered so as to support a different or absurd conclusion.
11. **T** F Both literal analogies and example arguments reason from cases, but the argument from example also generalizes about members of a category.
12. T **F** The text takes the position that all analogies are invalid.
13. **T** F One test of a literal analogy is to ask whether both cases have been presented accurately.
14. **T** F Figurative analogies can help an audience to visualize a situation or problem.
15. T **F** Narrative is distinct from argument, and should not be used to advance an argument.
16. **T** F Narrative has the capacity to render an idea plausible by placing it in the stream of the audience's experience.
17. T **F** In determining an author's point or claim in a narrative, we should disregard the protagonist's motives.

Multiple Choice

1. An analogy that compares relationships rather than cases.
    a. literal analogy
    b. contrasting analogy
    c. *a fortiori* argument
    d. judicial analogy
    <u>e.</u> figurative analogy

Chapter 14   Analogies, Examples, Metonymy, and Narratives

2. An analogy that affirms that what is true of its evidence case is even more likely or even less likely to be true of its conclusion case.
   - a. literal analogy
   - b. contrasting analogy
   - <u>c.</u> *a fortiori* argument
   - d. judicial analogy
   - e. figurative analogy

3. The statement, "Similar cases should be treated similarly" is called the
   - a. rule of charity
   - <u>b.</u> rule of justice
   - c. equal treatment principle
   - d. rule of similar cases
   - e. principle of judicial similarity

4. An analogy that insists on similar treatment for people, ideas, or institutions in similar circumstances.
   - a. literal analogy
   - b. contrasting analogy
   - <u>c.</u> judicial analogy
   - d. figurative analogy
   - e. *a fortiori* argument

5. A test of literal analogies is
   - a. Are the two cases dissimilar in some critical respect?
   - b. Is there proof for the analogy?
   - c. Are the two cases presented accurately?
   - d. All of the above are tests of literal analogies.
   - <u>e.</u> Items a and c are both tests of literal analogies.

6. A test of the argument from example is
   - a. Is the example typical of the category?
   - b. Is the example reported accurately?
   - c. Is a counter-example available?
   - <u>d.</u> All of the above are tests of the argument from example.
   - e. Items a and b are the only tests of the argument from example in this list.

7. Tests of narrative argument include
   - a. credibility
   - b. recency
   - c. coherence
   - d. fidelity
   - <u>e.</u> c and d

Terminology

1. Affirms that what is true of its evidence case is even more likely or even less likely to be true of its conclusion case. **a *fortiori* argument**

2. Insists on similar treatment for people, ideas, or institutions in similar circumstances. **judicial analogy**

3. Compares things that are not actually similar. **figurative analogy**

4. Affirms, in the conclusion, something as generally true about a class of objects rather than about a single member of a group. **argument from example**

5. A direct comparison between two allegedly similar items or cases. **literal analogy**

6. In a literal analogy, a familiar or widely established instance. **evidence case**

7. In a literal analogy, an instance about which a claim is being made. **conclusion case**

8. The claim that an exception should be made to the rule that similar cases should be treated similarly. **special pleading**

9. In a figurative analogy, the familiar relationship between two objects that is used as support for the conclusion. **evidence relationship**

10. An argument that draws a conclusion about an entire class of objects or events based on a particular instance, or limited number of instances. **argument from example**

11. The use of one object to represent another associated object, or of a single attribute to represent a complex object. **metonymy**

12. Two tests of narrative argument that consider factors both internal and external to the story's plot. **coherence and fidelity**

Short Answer

1. Provide three tests of literal analogies.
    1. **Are the cases compared dissimilar in some critical respect?**
    2. **Has the evidence case been described accurately?**
    3. **Are there any relevant counter-examples?**

2. Provide the connective for a judicial analogy.
    Similar cases should be treated similarly.

3. Provide three tests of figurative analogies.
    1. **Is the analogy advanced as illustration or argument?**
    2. **Does the figurative analogy appear without other arguments or evidence?**
    3. **Is the evidence relationship actually similar to the conclusion relationship?**

4. Provide three tests of the argument from example.
    1. **Is the example presented and interpreted accurately?**
    2. **Does the example represent the population?**
    3. **Is there a significant counter-example?**

Application

A. There are two analogies in the following argument.

   a. Name each analogy by type.

   b. Provide and label the evidence and conclusion cases or relationships for each.

   c. Provide the conclusion for each.

   We must save ourselves while there is still time and reject all forms of moral pluralism and relativism, which threaten our very survival. The Roman Empire provides us with a case that proves this contention. The United States is in so many ways like Rome just before its fall: morally careless and materialistic. These tendencies, which led to the decline of Rome, are even more strongly exhibited in our wealthy, self-centered society, so we are headed for a great moral disaster. Like the *Titanic*, that supposedly unsinkable ship, US society is headed toward the iceberg of moral pluralism, and like that great ship, we will be sunk if we don't reject moral pluralism.

   First analogy:

   a. Type: *a fortiori* argument

   b. Evidence case: Rome

   Conclusion case: United States

   c. Conclusion: We are headed for a great moral disaster.

   Second analogy:

   a. Type: figurative analogy

   b. Evidence relationship: *Titanic* / iceberg

   Conclusion relationship: US society / moral pluralism

   c. We will be sunk if we don't reject moral pluralism.

B. Identify the following analogies by type:

   1. Black holes in the universe suck into their centers everything within reach of their irresistible field of force. The Mars candy company is a black hole in the universe of packaged food corporations, swallowing smaller companies whole, without allowing even a single lumen of information to escape. (lumen = unit of light) **figurative analogy**

   2. If we have laws to protect us against fraud by manufacturers, then it is even more important that we have laws to protect us against fraud by politicians. Thus, this bill holding candidates accountable for promises they made during their campaigns deserves your support. ***a fortiori* argument**

   3. Korea has the same work ethic as Japan, and the same genius for reading market trends. Thus, I am certain we can expect Korea to become a leader in the international consumer goods market. **simple literal analogy**

   4. Why should he be exempted from paying the parking ticket just because he is a judge? I had to pay for mine, and he should have to pay for his! **judicial analogy**

C. For the following figurative analogy, provide the evidence and conclusion relationships.

Drugs are a terrible, life-threatening illness in our nation. Like a dread illness in our physical bodies, they must be attacked with every resource we have available before they cause our nation's final destruction.

Evidence relationship: dread illness / body

Conclusion relationship: drugs / nation

Chapter 15
Reasoning about Causes

EXERCISES

A. For each of the following hypothesis arguments, identify the observation(s) raising a causal question. Provide in your own words the causal question that arises out of the observation(s). Identify the hypothesis, and, if present, any additional evidence advanced in its support.

[Students are asked to list all observations, but should also be encouraged to identify the specific circumstance in each argument that needs explanation.]

1. Friday's accident was the first crash of the Air Force's newest stealth bomber. Surviving crew members say they observed a large flock of birds in the vicinity of the aircraft just before it crashed. It is speculated that the birds were sucked into the powerful engines of the bomber, causing it to crash.

Observations: The plane's crash is primary, because it is what must be explained. The crew's observation of a flock of birds could also be listed here, but fits better under supporting evidence.

Question: What caused the plane to crash?

[Note: The question should not anticipate the hypothesis by mentioning the birds. Thus, questions such as, "Did the birds cause the plane to crash?" are not properly phrased.]

Hypothesis: The birds were sucked into the powerful engines of the bomber, causing it to crash.

Supporting evidence: Testimony of surviving crew members.

Tests: The hypothesis is *adequate* if birds would be sufficient to explain such a crash. In fact, they would be sufficient, based on *analogous cases* in which this agency has caused such accidents. There may be an *alternative hypothesis* connected to the fact that the affected plane was relatively new and untested.

2. The Denver Mint, where most US coins are produced, has reduced its production by nearly 75 percent due to a lack of demand by banks and businesses for new coins. The obvious question is, "Why is demand for coins so low?" Two reasons have been suggested by the Mint's director, both of which have to do with the weak economy. The first is that consumers are simply spending less, which means there is lower demand for coins in cash registers. The second reason is that billions of coins have re-entered circulation as cash-strapped families and individuals return accumulated coins to banks in exchange for paper currency. This double effect of lower demand for coins and an increase of coins in circulation has driven down demand for new coins from the mint.

Observations: 75 percent reduction in production of new coins at Denver Mint; banks and businesses requesting fewer new coins.

Question: Why is demand for new coins so low?

Hypothesis: The weak economy is causing consumers to spend less, so *lower demand* for coins in cash registers. And, *increased supply* as billions of coins have re-entered circulation.

Supporting evidence: There is no additional evidence here, but there is some additional reasoning about the effect of the economy on families (they are exchanging coins for currency) and businesses (they are experiencing reduced sales, and thus less need for coins).

3. More than twenty whales beached themselves in the Canary Islands in 1989. Twelve more whales beached themselves along the coast of Greece in 1996. Similar incidents involving pilot whales have recently been reported in Oregon. In Hawaii more than two hundred bottle-nosed whales stranded themselves in 2005. Hundreds of pilot whales beached themselves in Antarctica in March 2009. The whales showed strange symptoms such as internal bleeding and brain damage. The Navy had been testing deep sea sonar devices in each of these areas prior to the beachings. That testing is the likely cause of these otherwise mysterious incidents. The 250-decibel sonar is so powerful that it can rupture blood vessels in the whales' brains, destroying their ability to navigate or killing them outright.

Observation: Whales beaching themselves in the Canary Islands; along the coast of Greece; and in Oregon, Hawaii, and Antarctica.

Question: Why have whales beached themselves at various places around the world over the past twenty years?

Hypothesis: Naval testing of 250-decibel sonar, so powerful that it can rupture blood vessels in the whales' brains, destroyed their ability to navigate or killed them outright.

Additional evidence: (1) The whales showed strange symptoms such as internal bleeding and brain damage. (2) The Navy had been testing deep sea sonar devices in each of these areas prior to the beachings.

4. Psychologists and sociologists report that we are becoming less trustful of other people. A variety of studies have indicated a dramatic increase in suspicion of outsiders and strangers over the past twenty years. What is causing this rising fear of others? Researchers point to two important causal factors. The first is that more of us now live in cities, where fears are always higher in comparison to rural areas. People living in rural communities feel closer connections to those around them. The other cause appears to be heavy media reporting of terrorism, disasters, and violent crime, which feeds the idea that the world is an increasingly dangerous place.

Observation: We are becoming less trustful of other people; a dramatic increase in suspicion of outsiders and strangers has occurred over the past twenty years.

Question: What is causing this rising fear of others?

Hypothesis: More people now live in cities where fears are always elevated; and heavy media reporting of terrorism, disasters, and violent crime feeds those fears.

Supporting evidence: None offered, though it is noted that people living in rural communities feel closer connections to those around them, and media feed the idea that the world is an increasingly dangerous place.

5. The United States will soon face a shortage of nearly ninety thousand doctors, mostly in family practice and primary care. Sixty million people in the US already live in regions experiencing a shortage of family physicians. Legislating mandatory medical care will not fix the doctor shortage: we will still face a medical crisis in this country. The primary cause of the current shortage of family practice physicians is the tendency of large teaching hospitals to encourage residents into lucrative and high-prestige specialties such as orthopedics and neurology. A review of recent medical school grads revealed that only 15 percent had selected family medicine as a specialty. Even fewer reported being encouraged to take this path through residency.

Observation: The United States will soon face a shortage of nearly ninety thousand doctors, mostly in family practice and primary care. Sixty million people in the US already live in regions experiencing a shortage of family physicians. Legislating mandatory medical care will not fix the doctor shortage: we will still face a medical crisis in this country.

Question: Why is the United States facing a shortage of doctors?

Hypothesis: The primary cause of the current shortage of family practice physicians is the tendency of large teaching hospitals to encourage residents into lucrative and high-prestige specialties such as orthopedics and neurology.

Supporting evidence: A review of recent medical school grads revealed that only 15 percent had selected family medicine as a specialty. Even fewer reported being encouraged to take this path through residency.

B. In the following examples, rival hypotheses are advanced to explain the same phenomenon. What are the alternative hypotheses in each case? How might they be tested to determine which one is more reasonable?

1. Once the breadbasket of the Middle East, Iraq is rapidly turning into a dust bowl reminiscent of the Plains states during our own Great Depression. Dust storms choke residents and deprive crops of sunlight. Different explanations for this stunning development are heard inside the country. To the average Iraqi the dust storms are the result of God's anger with the people of Iraq for ongoing violence and corruption. Agricultural experts studying the problem, however, note that two years of drought have followed years of warfare and resulting mismanagement of croplands. The nation no longer produces the large grain harvests it once did. For the first time Iraq will have to import 80 percent of its food this year. The damage to Iraq's land, water supplies, and agricultural production could take a decade or more to reverse.

Hypothesis 1: The dust storms are the result of God's anger with the people of Iraq for ongoing violence and corruption.

Hypothesis 2: Two years of drought have followed years of warfare and resulting mismanagement of croplands.

These two hypotheses refer to two very different types of causes, one testable, the other not. The second hypothesis offers a physical cause—drought and warfare—with measurements of precipitation and comparisons to pre-war productivity possible. The first hypothesis is based in faith commitments, and is thus not subject to external or observational tests. Agency is inaccessible in the second hypothesis.

2. Psychologists and counselors have noted a dramatic increase in the number of young people reporting feelings of jealousy in relationships. They speculated that fragmented families had led people in their teens and twenties to feel more threatened about intrusions on friendships and romantic relationships, but a recent study at the University of Guelph in Canada suggests a different cause. The study concluded that one of the unanticipated effects of the social networking site Facebook is to stir jealous feelings in its young users. Posts by those with whom they are romantically involved often suggest the existence of other relationships or interests. The result is that relationships often are undermined by feelings of suspicion and mistrust, and by a compulsive effort to attain more information.

Hypothesis 1: Fragmented families lead people in their teens and twenties to feel more threatened about intrusions on friendships and romantic relationships.

Hypothesis 2: The social networking site Facebook stirs jealous feelings in its young users by suggesting the existence of rival relationships, and creating a compulsive effort to attain more information.

These hypotheses may be complementary, the second one creating a more complete picture of the current social situation for many teens. However, the second hypothesis, because it is rooted in a study of social networking sites and their effects, and because it identifies a specific agency that might be tested by comparing teens who use the site with teens who do not, provides a more specific and adequate causal account. Certainly the relationship between specific cause and effect is more evident in the second hypothesis.

3. PepsiCo has just created its own music company called QMusic in China. Why would a soft drink company want to own and operate a music recording and distribution system in that country? The reason appears to be that this move allows PepsiCo to create and promote its own music stars, who can then be employed in major ad campaigns without the enormous cost of paying established stars. The company learned this lesson the hard way by working with overpaid and sometimes controversial superstars in the United States. The company's official reason for the move is the need to diversify in a rapidly changing economy.

Hypothesis 1: This move allows PepsiCo to create and promote its own music stars, who can then be employed in major ad campaigns without the enormous cost of paying established stars.

Hypothesis 2: The company made the move because it perceived a need to diversify in a rapidly changing economy.

The hypothesis testing suggested in the example itself points to prior knowledge of the relationships among the soft-drink, music, and advertising industries. Thus, hypothesis 1 refers to analogous cases in the US. The second hypothesis is dismissed as a public relations strategy that offers no agency for testing and that appears inadequate to account for PepsiCo's specific decisions.

4. The US explanation for dropping atomic bombs on the cities of Hiroshima and Nagasaki is that the action was needed to end the war and prevent the deaths of millions of additional Japanese citizens and soldiers on both sides. In Japanese textbooks the action is explained as America's effort to show the world that it would be willing to use nuclear weapons against its enemies—notably China and the Soviet Union—in the new era of the Cold War.

Rival hypotheses: Dropping atomic bombs on Hiroshima and Nagasaki was the United States's effort (1) to end the war and prevent the deaths of millions of additional Japanese citizens and soldiers on both sides or (2) to show the world that it would be willing to use nuclear weapons against its enemies—notably China and the Soviet Union—in the new era of the Cold War.

Tests: There is no clear test that would resolve this issue, though we could certainly ask whether a third alternative hypothesis better explains the facts—perhaps in this case a blending of the two rival hypotheses.

Another possible test is analogous cases. Did the US actually employ nuclear weapons—even smaller "tactical" nuclear weapons—in any other situation with the goal of ending a conflict and preventing a disastrous consequence? These weapons were not used during the Korean conflict, to end the long conflict in Vietnam, during the Cold War, or in the midst of the Cuban Missile Crisis. This test might suggest that the single use at the end of World War II was in some respects symbolic, thus supporting hypothesis 2.

5. Some people have attributed the so-called face on Mars to the construction activities of an intelligent alien race, but photographic and geological evidence reveal that the face and other features in its vicinity are actually a typical set of Martian mesas, geological formations common to the planet.

Hypothesis 1: The construction activities of an intelligent alien race.

Hypothesis 2: Typical Martian mesas, geological formations common to the planet.

Like example 1, above, the first hypothesis advances an essentially untestable hypothesis with hidden agency. The second refers to causal agency in Martian geology and to analogous cases of other similar mesas.

C. For the following causal analogies, identify the contrast advanced as cause and that advanced as effect.

1. Mills University and State University attract students from similar backgrounds. The entering freshmen at each institution have about the same SAT scores. Why do Mills students, then, always have an easier time landing good jobs after graduation? I think it is because of the extensive internship programs at Mills—something almost entirely lacking at State. Therefore, State should institute such an internship program.

Contrast advanced as cause: internship programs

Contrast advanced as effect: Mills students' ease in locating jobs

Other possible causes: reputations of institutions, location of institutions, actual quality of education at Mills

2. Canada and the United States are both developed countries and in close proximity. Lower-income people in the US, however, are in worse health than poorer members of Canadian society. The only important difference between the two medical systems is that the US system is often unavailable to the poor and the unemployed.

Contrast advanced as cause: unavailability of US system to the poor and unemployed

Contrast advanced as effect: worse health among lower-income people in the US than among lower-income Canadians

3. By the end of the 1980s, more Vietnam veterans had committed suicide since the war ended than had died in the war. A 2013 study found Iraq War and Desert Storm veterans were more than twice as likely to commit suicide as civilians. Why is this? Most clinical psychologists now accept that the cause of the extraordinarily high suicide rate was PTSD, or post-traumatic stress disorder, a combination of depression and anxiety that results from extreme trauma. The widespread presence of this disorder in vets as compared with the general population was the only important difference between veterans and the rest of the adult population.

Contrast advanced as cause: widespread presence of PTSD among veterans as compared to the general population

Contrast advanced as effect: more veterans had committed suicide since the war ended than had died in the war; (implied) a higher suicide rate among veterans than in the general population

4. European and US teens report about the same level of sexual activity, but the pregnancy rate among European teens is much lower than among US teens. Comprehensive sex education for adolescents is mandatory in many European countries, including instruction in various forms of contraception. Comprehensive sex education is often unavailable to teens in the United States because of state and federal regulations. Experts believe the more thorough sex education in European schools contributes to a decrease in the teen pregnancy rate.

Contrast advanced as cause: mandatory, comprehensive sex education

Contrast advanced as effect: lower pregnancy rate

5. Do real estate agents exert as much effort selling your home as they do selling their own? Analysis of sales data on 100,000 homes in the Chicago area revealed that the 3,000 homes owned by real estate agents stayed on the market an average of ten days longer than the others and were sold for prices 3 percent or more above the prices of similar homes. This comparison suggests that agents were willing to wait longer to sell their own homes—presumably for a higher bidder to come along—and that they worked harder to obtain a higher final selling price. [Example based on report by Steven Levitt and Stephen Dubner, "Cracking the Real Estate Code," *Wired Magazine*, May 2005, 106–109.]

Contrast advanced as cause: Real estate agents were willing to wait longer to sell their own homes—presumably to a higher bidder—and worked harder to obtain a higher final selling price.

Contrast advanced as effect: Homes owned by real estate agents stay on the market longer than those owned by other people, and sell for a higher price than similar homes.

D. In the following examples, identify the causal generalization being advanced. What factor is identified as cause? What is the supposed effect? State whether you see any potential problems in the causal reasoning in each example.

1. Research involving 55 mice specially bred to develop Alzheimer's Disease revealed that caffeine can be effective in restoring memory. Mice with Alzheimer's given the equivalent of 500 milligrams of caffeine a day for eight weeks showed a memory equivalent to normal mice. Mice with normal memories given the same amount of caffeine did not show any increase in memory. Thus, the chemical can work to restore lost memory but not to improve normal memory.

Cause: caffeine

Effect: restoring memory

Possible problems: relatively small sample size, potentially different effects in mice and humans

2. A study of more than 4,500 students in fifth through eighth grades found that children who watch R-rated movies, which often portray high levels of smoking, were more than fifteen times more likely to try smoking than were children whose parents limited them to G and PG movies. [The Impact of Smoking in the Movies on Youth Smoking Levels," Campaign for Tobacco-Free Kids," http://www.tobaccofreekids.org/research/factsheets/pdf/0216.pdf (Accessed December 27, 2006).]

Cause: watching R-rated movies, which portray high levels of smoking

Effect: Children were more than fifteen times more likely to try smoking than were children whose parents limited them to G and PG movies.

Possible problems: A third variable might be a lack or parental guidance in the home that led to both R-rated movie viewing and smoking in children.

3. Two biologists at the University of Manitoba have demonstrated a striking correlation between practicing yoga and eating a healthy diet in a year-long study of 310 people. Some observers have speculated that, among yoga's other benefits, it stimulates an appetite for more wholesome foods.

Cause: practicing yoga

Effect: eating healthy food

Possible problems: Clearly, a third variable is at work here: interest in health.

E. Explain how argument from sign is employed in the following examples. Which signs are taken as leading back to a likely cause? What is that cause?

1. While US and European interests are focused on the Middle East, Western nations need to be alert to the fact that China is rapidly developing as a major military power. In 2007 the People's Republic launched a missile that destroyed one of its own communication satellites, a remarkable technological achievement of which the Chinese did not inform other countries for two weeks. Satellite imagery has revealed an enormous underground navel base on the Chinese island of Hainan. The apparent purpose of this base is to launch navel operations in the Pacific. Finally, in January 2010, China conducted an advanced missile-defense test.

Sign: China's development of military facilities and capacities

Cause: China is emerging as a major military power.

2. The mental health of children from families in which a parent is or may be deployed to a combat zone appears to be a looming issue around military bases. Over the past five years there has been a dramatic increase in depression and anxiety disorders among children of military personnel. Teachers on military bases report that their students show symptoms of sleep deprivation. Counselors also have noted that military children frequently express deep anxiety bordering on obsession regarding parents who have been deployed to combat zones.

Sign: a dramatic increase in mental health disturbances among children of military personnel

Cause: negative effects of parental deployment to combat zones on children of military parents

3. Sales of large pickup trucks have risen by more than 20 percent in the past year. We know that pickup sales are a good indicator, not just that the building trades are rebounding, but that consumer confidence is also improving. When builders have plenty of work, they buy new pickups. Thus, improvement in the building trades means improved pickup sales. The building trades are themselves an excellent predictor of consumer confidence, so we can say that improved pickup sales are a reliable indicator of consumer confidence.

Sign: Sales of large pickup trucks

Cause: Improvements in building trade, more generally improvement in consumer confidence

QUIZZES

Quiz #1

1. Two methods of proving cause are discussed in Chapter 15. One method is analogy. The other method is used to establish cause in the following hypothesis argument. What is this method called?

   Murders are committed out of a desire for revenge, extreme need, or mental derangement. My client could not have been seeking revenge, is not needy, and is in a sound mental state. Thus, he could not have killed Mr. Jones. **enumeration**

2. Identify the observation, question, hypothesis, and additional evidence in the following argument.

   Teen suicides have declined 25 percent since the early 1990s. Sociologists speculate that improved treatment of teen depression and efforts to reduce teen drug use are the main factors in the decline. A recent report on teen suicide by the American Academy of Pediatrics lends support to this conclusion.

   Observation: Teen suicides have declined 25 percent since the early 1990s.

   Question: Why have teen suicides been declining?

   Hypothesis: Improved treatment of teen depression and efforts to reduce teen drug use are the main factors in the decline.

   Supporting evidence: A recent report by the American Academy of Pediatrics lends support to this conclusion.

3. Reasoning *post hoc* is the name given to just one fallacy of causal generalization. Which test reveals the *post hoc* fallacy? **succession**

Quiz #2

1. One test of a causal generalization is succession. What are the other two?

   correlation and agency

2. The following causal generalization passes only one of the three tests of causal generalization arguments. Which one does it pass? What is alleged as cause and what as effect in the argument? Briefly explain specifically why the causal reasoning in this example might be flawed.

   An extensive test of more than five hundred highly successful business executives showed that the vast majority of these people, more than 80 percent, also have unusually well-developed vocabularies. It seems clear, then, that a large vocabulary ensures success in business.

   Cause: well-developed vocabulary

   Effect: business success

   Test the argument passes: correlation

   Potential problem in causal reasoning based on this one factor: failure to identify hidden third cause: education

TEST ITEMS

True or False

1. T **F** Reasoning from correlation alone is generally safe when constructing a causal generalization.
2. **T** F Arguing from succession alone is a risky way of doing causal reasoning.
3. **T** F Frequently, more than one hypothesis is advanced to explain an observation.
4. T **F** The absence of a clear causal agent in the hypothesis should lead to immediate rejection of the argument.
5. **T** F One step in generating a hypothesis is to generate its consequences on the assumption of its accuracy.
6. T **F** It is not likely that a hypothesis can be tested by reference to analogous cases.
7. **T** F One test of a hypothesis is to ask whether an alternative hypothesis would explain the observed events better.
8. T **F** Causal analogies—which argue cause by analogy—focus on dissimilarities as well as similarities between the cases compared.
9. **T** F Enumeration can be a valuable means of arguing for cause.
10. T **F** Arguing by correlation alone is an effective means of establishing causal generalizations.
11. **T** F Arguing from succession alone is also called the *post hoc* fallacy.
12. **T** F The test of succession seeks to ensure that an alleged effect preceded its cause.
13. **T** F One problem of reasoning from correlation alone is that a possible common cause of the correlated events might be overlooked.
14. T **F** The test of agency is one test of hypothesis reasoning, but not of causal generalization.
15. **T** F The philosopher Karl Popper claimed that a reasonable hypothesis should be falsifiable, or capable of being shown false.
16. T **F** A causal agent is a person who investigates causes of events.
17. **T** F The "rule of parsimony" suggests that the most reasonable hypothesis often is the simplest and least complex causal explanation.
18. T **F** The argument from sign allows us to reason from cause directly to effect, even before the effect occurs.
19. **T** F A fallible sign is an effect with more than one possible cause, though one cause is typical.
20. **T** F Causal claims can be established by reasoning from analogy and by reasoning from enumeration.
21. T **F** Reasoning from correlation alone is a reliable approach to causal reasoning.

Multiple Choice

1. Which of the following is *not* discussed in the text as a test of hypothesis arguments?
   a. adequacy of the hypothesis
   b. evident agency in the cause
   <u>c.</u> correlation of cause and effect
   d. in similar cases, similar hypotheses have been shown accurate
   e. possibility of alternative hypothesis

2. An argument that alleges a causal relationship between two categories of events.
   a. argument from cause
   b. conditional argument
   c. hypothesis argument
   <u>d.</u> causal generalization
   e. argument from sign

3. Which of the following is *not* discussed in the text as a test of causality in a causal generalization?
   <u>a.</u> adequacy of cause
   b. correlation of cause and effect
   c. succession of cause and effect
   d. agency
   e. all are discussed as tests of causality in causal generalizations

4. Attributing cause simply on the basis of events occurring together.
   a. arguing from succession alone
   b. arguing from agency alone
   <u>c.</u> arguing from correlation alone
   d. arguing for causal hypothesis
   e. arguing *post hoc*

5. Arguing for cause strictly on the basis of succession.
   a. hypothesis testing
   b. proving cause by analogy
   c. arguing from correlation alone
   d. proving cause by enumeration
   <u>e.</u> arguing *post hoc*

Terminology

1. Attributing cause simply on the basis of one event's preceding another. **arguing from succession alone, or *post hoc* fallacy**

2. A factor that could produce an observed effect. **causal agent**

3. An explanatory statement affirming that one event has caused another. **hypothesis**

4. A quality achieved when a correlation between events cannot be explained on the basis of simple coincidence. **significance**

5. Attributing cause simply on the basis of events occurring together. **arguing from correlation alone**

6. A parallel group to the test group in which a suspected cause has been withheld or eliminated. **control group**

Short Answer

1. Identify the four steps involved in formulating and testing a hypothesis.

   1. Suggest a testable hypothesis.

   2. Generate the consequences of the hypothesis on the assumption of its accuracy.

   3. Compare actual observations to the generated consequences.

   4. Accept, modify, or reject the hypothesis.

2. Provide three tests of the hypothesis argument.

   1. Does the hypothesis account adequately for the event (including the question of whether the hypothesis involves a causal agent that is capable of bringing about the observed effects)?

   2. Has a similar hypothesis been shown to be accurate in analogous cases?

   3. Is there an alternative hypothesis that better explains the observed events?

3. Provide three tests specific to the causal generalization.

   1. Are the two events correlated?

   2. Does the alleged cause consistently precede the effect?

   3. Does the cause include an agent that could bring about the effect?

4. Identify the type of reasoning used to establish cause in the following:

   You're just as smart as your sister, but you don't study. That's why she works for IBM, and you're still making fries at Burger Heaven.

   establishing cause by analogy

5. Describe the method of proving cause by enumeration.

   1. Set out all plausible options.

   2. Eliminate options convincingly.

Application

1. Explain what is occurring in the following causal argument. What type of causal reasoning—hypothesis or causal generalization—is employed? Suggest a possible weakness with or an answer to the argument based on the appropriate tests.

> Heavy rainfall last April resulted in eight million gallons of raw sewage being spilled into the Grand River from the Grand Rapids sewage treatment facility. Doctors in Grand Rapids report that, since the spill, they have seen a sharp increase in giardia—a bacterial infection that causes intestinal distress. Many doctors have suggested that new cases of the disease have resulted from people swimming in the contaminated river.

Hypothesis is advanced to explain observations. If any of the people who contracted giardia did not swim in the river, an alternative hypothesis might be necessary. In this event, a simple alteration such as *any* contact with the water would strengthen the hypothesis.

Chapter 16
Moral and Practical Arguments

EXERCISES

A. Identify the specific type of argument advanced in each of the following examples.

1. Five billion people on earth have no access to the Internet. That's why our plan to place balloons in the stratosphere to connect everyone on Earth to the Internet is so urgent. **argument from quantity**

2. The demand for euthanasia is most pronounced where social support networks are weakest, and where medical care is expensive and hard to obtain. This would suggest that if euthanasia were widely legalized it would be sought out by those who feel isolated and lack resources. Thus, euthanasia is not a morally grounded solution to human suffering. **argument from principle**

3. In a surprising and helpful development for the wind power industry, a majority of residents living in the vicinity of wind farms say they like the appearance of gigantic turbines. The enormous, slowly rotating blades and stately white towers are said to bring an air of majesty and tranquility to the landscape. **The *quality* argument's concern for aesthetic response to the windmills is emphasized. The term "majority" does also suggest an appeal to quantity.**

4. The World Wildlife Fund estimates that producing a single cup of latte requires two hundred liters of water. This figure takes into consideration the water used to grow the coffee, manufacture the cup and lid, produce the milk in the drink, and then brew the coffee. This number must be multiplied by the enormous number of lattes consumed each day. Practicing better conservation measures is the key to enjoying a cup of coffee without threatening our water supply. **The emphasis is on quantity considerations, but there is also a concern for the pragmatic issue of depleting the water supply.**

5. Green roofs—roofs planted with grass, vegetables, and flowering plants—are the wave of the future, and for good reason. They decrease rain runoff, improve the energy efficiency of buildings, improve the urban landscape, and can even serve as a source of food. **A series of pragmatic considerations provides the basis for this argument.**

6. Bryce Canyon must be preserved as a wilderness area because developing the canyon would threaten the last remaining bristlecone pines, the rarest and oldest trees on earth. **argument from quality**

7. Wilderness areas in the United States should be preserved, not just because they are beautiful, but for a less well-recognized reason—they are intimately tied to the health of the people, who benefit physically from being outside. **Though the quality concern for preserving something beautiful is suggested, the pragmatic issue of health provides the basis for this argument.**

8. Autism research is being hindered by a shortage of human brain matter for study. Thus, the regulations governing the use of human tissue samples in research should be revised to make more samples available for research purposes. **pragmatic argument**

9. Cloning a mammoth is no longer a matter of technology, but of time, money, and will. We certainly know how to do it, but should we? Mammoths, like elephants, were highly social animals. We would clone one to satisfy our own curiosity, but that would not be fair to the animal itself, which would live out a lonely existence, isolated and in captivity. **Here the principle issue of fairness to an animal is the foundation of the argument.**

10. The Planetary Science Division of NASA says more than ten thousand large asteroids and four thousand small asteroids have been detected in the observable solar system. More than one thousand of these objects are each a kilometer in diameter, large enough to destroy human life on earth. While a few asteroids in our vicinity may not pose much of a threat, the laws of probability clearly suggest that thousands do. It's time we took seriously the threat posed to our safety by such enormous numbers of potentially deadly asteroids. **argument from quantity**

11. Wall Street executives were paid $18 billion in bonuses the same year the government bailed out many big banks and finance companies. This is simply unconscionable. It violates the average person's sense of right and wrong. **A principle is being invoked—our fundamental sense of right and wrong.**

12. The National Parks receive more than four hundred million visitors a year, more than attend NFL, NASCAR, the NBA, and Major League Baseball events combined. Thus, the parks system deserves our financial support. **Quantity is the basis for action here.**

13. Dean Victor Gold, of Loyola Law School in Los Angeles, explained the school's decision to reduce the number of new admissions: "Reality has caught up to higher education . . . . We have a moral obligation not to just take tuition dollars and then turn a blind eye when our graduates can't find jobs." [Jason Song, "Faced with Job Complaints, Loyola Law School Accepting Fewer Students," *Los Angeles Times,* August 19, 2013, http://www.latimes.com/news/local/la-me-loyola-law-20130819,0,2313212.story (Accessed August 20, 2013).] **argument from principle**

14. As a young man, Teddy Roosevelt climbed the Matterhorn and saw no wildlife. He came to believe that what made the United States landscape unique was the presence of wildlife in our wilderness areas. He sought to create the National Wildlife Preserve for one reason—to preserve the irreplaceable treasure of our wild places and wild animals. **Quality argument is noted as Roosevelt's motive.**

15. Arming some school employees to guard against shooters coming into schools is more dangerous than the risk of a shooter. **pragmatic argument**

B. Which test of the pragmatic argument has been applied in the following example?

Those who are lobbying for embryonic stem cell research are, in fact, hindering progress into stem cell research. That is, they are hurting their own cause. Let me explain. The protest against embryonic stem cells is founded on moral issues regarding the status of the embryo. Many biologists believe that it is not necessary to use embryos at all, because adult stem cells are available in bone marrow and other places in the body. The problem for researchers is that adult stem cells do not show the plasticity of embryo cells; that is, they are not capable of differentiating into different kinds of cells, but are programmed to become only one type of cell. Many experts agree that further research will allow scientists to induce plasticity in adult stem cells, thus completely eliminating the need for embryonic stem cells. Here's the irony: the controversy generated by current lobbying for the use of embryonic stem cells is drawing attention and support away from research into inducing plasticity in adult stem cells.

test of unintended consequences

C. The following are arguments based on principles. For each example, state the moral principle being invoked. In addition, identify the action that is considered to be a violation of the principle.

1. Only about one in ten of those killed in US pilotless drone strikes is a targeted combatant. Our obligation to protect the lives of innocent civilians means that our current policies concerning pilotless drones in combat are unacceptable.

Moral obligation to protect the lives of the innocent.

Pilotless drone strikes.

2. Pharmaceutical companies giving presents to medical students in order to convince them to prescribe company drugs after they graduate violates the ethical principle that corporate money should not play a role in shaping medical curricula.

Moral principle that corporate money should not play a role in shaping medical curricula.

Pharmaceutical companies giving gifts to medical students.

3. Some robots and computers are intelligent enough to be self-aware, and thus qualify as machine persons. We have a duty to protect their rights as persons. Thus, arbitrarily turning off an intelligent machine is immoral.

Moral duty to protect the rights of persons.

Arbitrarily turning off an intelligent machine.

4. Keeping a prisoner in solitary confinement is a violation of the constitutional guarantee of protection from cruel and unusual punishment.

Constitutional protection against cruel and unusual punishment.

Keeping a prisoner in solitary confinement.

5. It is wrong to deny the right to marry to gay people. Such a prohibition violates a fundamental human right to seek happiness.

Right to seek happiness.

Denying the right to marry to gay people.

6. The proposal that parents should be allowed to "design" their children by genetic engineering violates the moral limit on tampering with nature.

Moral limit on tampering with nature.

Parents being allowed to "design" their children.

7. The US has a moral obligation to promote human rights in other countries through its trade policies and diplomatic activities.

Promoting human rights in other countries.

Enacting trade policies and pursuing diplomatic activities.

8. A recognizable model of a human face can now be constructed from DNA left on cigarette butts, chewing gum, or saliva on a coffee cup. This procedure—which has been successfully performed in at least one college art class—raises privacy concerns.

Right to privacy.

Reconstructing model of the human face from found DNA.

TEST ITEMS

True or False

1. <u>T</u> F Pragmatic arguments are concerned with the consequences of proposed actions.
2. <u>T</u> F One test of the pragmatic argument is to ask whether the action in question is likely to have the predicted consequences.
3. T <u>F</u> "Does the proposed action violate an important principle?" is a test of the argument from quality.
4. <u>T</u> F In testing pragmatic arguments, you should ask whether another course of action would be more advantageous than the proposed action.
5. <u>T</u> F The strategy of comparative advantages is frequently used in controversies in which alternative solutions to a problem are being considered.
6. T <u>F</u> An argument that discourages a course of action on the basis of a value is probably an argument from quantity.
7. <u>T</u> F Some arguments from principle derive from rights such as the right of free speech.
8. T <u>F</u> The argument from principle focuses attention on the rare, beautiful, or irreplaceable.
9. <u>T</u> F The response to an argument from principle often comes in the form of a pragmatic argument.
10. <u>T</u> F The argument from quantity assumes that big numbers suggest significance and small numbers suggest insignificance.

Multiple Choice

1. An argument that recommends or discourages a course of action on the basis of its consequences.
    - <u>a.</u>   pragmatic argument
    - b.   argument from quality
    - c.   argument from quantity
    - d.   argument from principle
    - e.   person/act argument

2. An argument that expresses a preference for numerical considerations, such as abundance and longevity, or a disregard for things that do not exhibit these characteristics.
    - a.   pragmatic argument
    - b.   argument from quality
    - <u>c.</u>   argument from quantity
    - d.   argument from principle
    - e.   person/act argument

3. An argument that expresses a preference for the unique, the beautiful, the rare, or the unusual.
    - a.   pragmatic argument
    - <u>b.</u>   argument from quality
    - c.   argument from quantity
    - d.   argument from principle
    - e.   person/act argument

4. An argument that affirms that we should abide by values, principles, and duties, and avoid actions that violate the same.
    - a.   pragmatic argument
    - b.   argument from quality
    - c.   argument from quantity
    - <u>d.</u>   argument from principle
    - e.   person/act argument

Terminology

1. An argument that recommends or discourages a course of action on the basis of its consequences. **pragmatic argument**

2. An argument that expresses a preference for numerical considerations such as abundance and longevity, or a disregard for things that do not exhibit these characteristics. **argument from quantity**

3. An argument that expresses a preference for the unique, the beautiful, the rare, or the unusual. **argument from quality**

4. An argument that affirms that we should abide by values, principles, and duties, and avoid actions that violate the same. **argument from principle**

Short Answer

1. Provide any two tests of the pragmatic argument.
   1. **Is the action in question likely to have the suggested consequences?**
   2. **Will the proposed argument have serious undesirable consequences?**
   3. **Does the proposed course of action violate an important principle?**

2. Provide any two tests of the arguments from principle.
   1. **Is the principle relevant to this issue?**
   2. **Is the principle in question violated by the proposed action?**
   3. **Do other considerations outweigh this principle?**

3. Identify two tests of the argument from quantity.
   1. **Is the quantity claim accurate?**
   2. **Are other considerations more important than quantity?**

4. Provide any two tests of the argument from quality.
   1. **Is the indicated quality actually present?**
   2. **Is the quality more clearly represented elsewhere?**
   3. **Do other concerns outweigh this quality?**

Application

Identify the following arguments, strategies, or fallacies by type.

1. We should give Jones the new hybrid car because it would save money in the sales division if she had a more economical car. **pragmatic argument**

2. We should give Jones the new car because we have a moral obligation to help out our employees who are struggling financially. **argument from principle**

3. AIDS testing should be required of all people applying for life insurance, because such testing has the backing of the vast majority of people in the United States. **argument from quantity**

4. Cultural relativism is an attractive philosophy to many people. However, few philosophers accept relativism as an adequate moral foundation. **argument from quantity: The small number of philosophers endorsing the idea is used as a reason to condemn it.**

5. Though you may disagree with what George has to say, he has a right to freedom of speech just like anyone else, and so should be allowed to talk. **argument from principle**

6. Testing everyone for AIDS should *not* be adopted as a policy because such testing represents a violation of the right to privacy. **argument from principle**

7. We should promote Higgins because he has been with the company longer than anyone else. **argument from quantity**

8. Bennington should be selected as the party's candidate for one simple reason—she's the best qualified candidate. **argument from quality**

9. Despite parental concerns, flu shots should be required of all school children, as the requirement would radically reduce the incidence of illness in the schools. **pragmatic argument**

10. Foreign language requirements often are not popular with college students, but benefits such as greater cultural awareness and greater potential for future employment fulfill good educational objectives. **pragmatic argument**

11. Linguists are working to restore and preserve several Native American languages. The head of the project, Dr. Alec Grossinger, defended the program as "an effort to prevent the loss of unusual and irreplaceable elements of disappearing cultures." **argument from quality**

12. Hispanic voters in Miami and Dade counties are now the largest and thus most important voting block, with over five million members in these two counties alone. **argument from quantity**

13. Australian pearls are the rarest and most beautiful pearls in the world. When making your jewelry selection, don't settle for ordinary pearls. **argument from quality**

Chapter 17
Essential Nature Arguments

EXERCISES

A. Identify the specific essential nature argument advanced in each of the following examples.

1. It is clear from the design of an assault rifle that it has a military purpose, and thus should not be easily available to members of the general public. The very form of these weapons suggests that they are not for civilian uses such as hunting. **argument from function, in this case based on form**

2. The founders of this nation believed that the citizen soldier was the best person to defend the country. A volunteer army thus violates their vision for national defense. **argument from intent**

3. The central goal of a public health system is to keep people well, not to make a profit. Thus, our current system of "health for sale to the highest bidders" should be overhauled radically to reflect its guiding purpose. **argument from function**

4. Online courses change something in the very essence of education—the face-to-face mentoring presence of the expert teacher is removed and replaced with text and a two-dimensional representation. Education is not at its core about the delivery of information—as some self-styled experts suggest—but the modeling of trained critical awareness and the careful analysis of complex issues. Online courses substitute the former for the latter. **argument from function**

5. To interpret this poem correctly we must understand that the author intended it as a Marxist statement about the ongoing class struggle and the eventual triumph of the working class. Seeing it as a statement about personal struggle and overcoming obstacles may be meaningful to you, but that is not what the poem is about. **argument from intent**

6. Christians should not give their children candy eggs and similar items as part of the Easter celebration. They should also refrain from throwing rice at weddings. Such symbols were originally signs of fertility in religious cults associated with fertility goddesses such as Ishtar, and therefore have no place in a Christian ceremony or celebration. **genetic argument**

7. A fully autonomous robot or drone making decisions in a combat situation changes the essence of warfare. Instead of human beings making the ethically complex decision regarding whether to kill other human beings, a machine is making those decisions based on an algorithm. War involves human agents taking real risks and weighing their own lives against the lives of others. This is no longer the case when robots and drones take over the fighting.
argument from function

8. The board of trustees has been critical of the boss, calling her insubordinate, self-centered, and aloof. As a twenty-year employee of the company, I know these charges about her character are not true. Her recent advocacy of raises for all staff members angered the board, but this action reveals a person who is caring and has her priorities straight. The fact that she will not stage company events to satisfy the board shows that she has courage under pressure. **person/act argument**

9. I favor allowing athletes to use performance-enhancing drugs. Everyone knows that sport is about pushing competition and performance to the highest level, which is precisely what these pharmaceuticals do. Why not allow athletes to compete at the peak of their abilities? **argument from the function of sport**

10. Keeping porpoises and dolphins in water parks violates their nature as intelligent and highly social animals. **argument from function**

11. The sports press has often covered up the misdeeds of celebrity sports figures. Its highly selective reporting cannot be excused as staying out of the players' private lives. Sports reporters reveal their own sexism when they ignore athletes' spousal abuse, and their disregard for law when they treat drug use as insignificant. **person/act argument, applied to group**

12. Human cloning deliberately severs a natural link between procreation and human sexual intercourse. This connection was established by the creator as part of the design of nature. It should not be broken through the artificial creation of human life. **argument from intent**

13. The Declaration of Independence sets out citizens' rights to life, liberty, and the pursuit of happiness. It is the proper role of government to care for the vulnerable and marginalized—to protect their lives and chances for happiness—including the elderly. Thus, ensuring medical care and housing for an increasingly aged society is a proper role of government, and not the obligation of private organizations or even of families. **argument from function, in this case based on prescription**

B. Provide an example of a work of art, a performance, a building, or an event that you consider to be creating a visual essential nature argument. Write a one- to two-page explanation of how the argument is constructed visually and the conclusion to which it leads.

ADDITIONAL EXERCISES

A. Identify the essential nature argument advanced in the following examples.

1. I don't like the way basketball is played today. All this showboating gets the game away from what the guys who originally put it together meant it to be: a sport emphasizing teamwork.

The second sentence suggests an argument from intent by placing emphasis on the originators of the game.

2. People simply weren't meant to take on the awesome responsibilities of making decisions about life and death. We are not God and do not have the capacity to know when someone else should live or die.

An argument from intent is suggested by the phrase, "People simply weren't meant to." The first sentence points to a divine plan for humankind that did not include making such decisions. The second sentence could be read as advancing an argument denying a function to human beings—deciding when someone else should live or die. The emphasis remains on what a higher authority intended for people.

3. It's downright criminal that city officials are using the new immigration laws to scare legal immigrants out of the city. The bill was supposed to ensure that legal immigrants could hold jobs in the city and to curtail the practice of employing illegal immigrants.

The second sentence advances an argument from function, though the purposes or intentions of the bill's authors are also implied in the phrase "was supposed to." The emphasis here remains on what the bill should function to do and on violations of that proper function.

4. The beat of rock music originally was the beat of music used in demon-worship rituals. Thus, rock music cannot escape condemnation as demonic.

A genetic argument is suggested here.

5. Schools are there to provide an education, not to provide material support for extracurricular activities. Because condoms are intended for use outside the schools, and because they have little or nothing to do with the school's educational functions, they should not be distributed by the schools.

Schools are affirmed as having a function, and are in the same sentence denied another function. Condoms are also said to have a proper function that is incommensurate with the educational purposes (functions) of schools.

TEST ITEMS

True or False

1. <u>T</u> F   In testing the genetic argument, it is important to balance a thing's current meanings or uses against its origins.
2. T <u>F</u>   The genetic argument finds essential nature to be revealed in an object's proper function.
3. <u>T</u> F   The argument from intent is especially important in controversies surrounding the interpretation of documents such as the Constitution.
4. <u>T</u> F   In testing the argument from function, it is important to ask whether function has been accurately assigned.
5. T <u>F</u>   Among the sources of function discussed in the text was the origin of an object or practice.
6. <u>T</u> F   Sometimes function is assigned on the basis of common understanding.
7. <u>T</u> F   In testing the person/act argument, we should ask whether the act in question is consistent with other acts attributed to an individual.
8. T <u>F</u>   The significance of a person's acts is clear, and does not require interpretation.
9. <u>T</u> F   Asking whether origin reveals essence is one test of the genetic argument.
10. <u>T</u> F   The argument from intent affirms that the essential nature of an object or document is revealed in the intended meaning of its authors or designers.
11. T <u>F</u>   The argument from function can be applied to social institutions, but not to naturally occurring phenomena.
12. <u>T</u> F   The person/act argument can be applied to groups as well as to individuals.
13. <u>T</u> F   A skyscraper may advance an argument visually.
14. T <u>F</u>   Photojournalism is a means of reporting a story, and is thus not a means of advancing an argument.

Multiple Choice

1. Which of the following is *not* discussed in the text as a possible response to the charge of inconsistency?

   a. The apparent inconsistency can be denied as being based on false or inaccurate claims.
   b. There is a reasonable way of resolving the inconsistency.
   <u>c.</u> The inconsistency is not serious.
   d. Show consistency between the allegedly inconsistent actions or statement.
   e. b and c

2. An argument that claims that origins reveal essential nature.
    <u>a.</u> genetic argument
    b. argument from intent
    c. argument from function
    d. person/act argument
    e. argument from inconsistency

3. An argument that affirms that essential nature is revealed in the intended meaning of authors or designers.
    a. argument from function
    <u>b.</u> argument from intent
    c. genetic argument
    d. intentional fallacy
    e. argument from inconsistency

4. Which of the following is *not* discussed in the text as a test of the argument from intent?
    a. Does the author's intent govern interpretation in this case?
    b. Is intent represented accurately?
    c. Do other considerations outweigh intent?
    d. Only items a and b are tests of the argument from intent.
    <u>e.</u> Items a, b, and c are tests of the argument from intent.

5. Which of the following is *not* discussed in the text as a source of function?
    a. prescription
    b. common understanding
    <u>c.</u> authority
    d. current need
    e. form

6. Which of the following is *not* discussed in the text as a test of the person/act argument?
    <u>a.</u> Is this individual's character generally well respected?
    b. Is it the case that the nature of the person is revealed in his or her acts?
    c. Are the observed acts consistent with other acts performed by this person?
    d. Has this act been interpreted accurately?
    e. All are tests of the person/act argument.

Terminology

Provide the correct term for the following definitions.

1. An argument that claims that origins reveal essential nature. **genetic argument**

2. An argument that affirms that essential nature is revealed in the intended meaning of authors or designers. **argument from intent**

Application

Identify the following arguments by type and suggest a weakness or response for each based on the appropriate tests.

1. Faculty at state universities should not wear caps and gowns to university functions, because this form of dress originated in the monasteries of Europe and reflects a religious preference.

   genetic argument

   Possible response: The origin and the present meaning of caps and gowns (ceremonial regalia) are related in a very limited way.

2. Don't use your desk as a stand for your aquarium—that's not what it's for.

   argument from function

   Possible response: Present need may dictate this use.

3. If you want to play that piece correctly, play it softly throughout. That's how Chopin himself played it after he wrote it.

   argument from intent

   Possible responses: Does Chopin's intent properly govern the interpretation of all of his music? Has Chopin's intent been accurately represented? Do present musical tastes outweigh intent?

4. I don't read the horoscope, since astrology originated as a pagan religious practice with satanic overtones.

   genetic argument

   Possible response: Present meanings or uses may outweigh origin.

5. The Drug Enforcement Agency can't be expected to provide counseling for drug users. It's set up to be a police force.

   argument from function

   Possible response: Function may change with current need.

6. The poem must be taken as a statement about the inherent tragedy of all human life, since the poet herself gave it this interpretation at a reading I attended.

   argument from intent

   Possible response: Intent of author does not dictate interpretation in all cases.

7. Mark is a great guy. Just look at all the times he's donated blood and visited children at the hospital.

   person/act argument

   Possible response: The act in question can be affirmed to be inconsistent with other acts.

Short Answer

1. Provide the two tests of the person/act argument.

    1. Has this act been interpreted accurately?

    2. Are the observed acts consistent with other acts by this person?

2. Provide three sources of function, with a brief explanation of each.

    1. Prescription: the function is written down somewhere that is considered official or authoritative.

    2. Common understanding: what the function of a thing is commonly taken to be.

    3. Form: the function of a thing derived from its appearance or form.

    4. Current need: function assigned on the basis of what is currently necessary.

3. Provide the assumption about the relationship between people and their acts that serves as the connective for the person/act argument.

    Acts reveal a person's nature.

4. Provide two tests of the person/act argument.

    1. Has this act been interpreted accurately?

    2. Are the observed acts consistent with other acts by this person?

5. Provide three tests of the genetic argument.

    1. Does origin reveal essence?

    2. Is the origin account accurate?

    3. Are present meanings or uses more important than origin?

6. Provide three tests of the argument from intent.

    1. Does the author's intent govern interpretation in this case?

    2. Has the intent been represented accurately?

    3. Do other considerations outweigh intent?

Chapter 18
Fallacies and Appeals

EXERCISES

A. Identify any fallacies or potential fallacies in the following examples.

1. I don't believe in a personal God, but this does not mean that the vast plan that is unfolding on the earth is any less meaningful. We need to assist the growth of a world mind that developments such as the Internet are bringing about. **question begging**

2. There is no way I would condone his use of campaign funds to pay for vacations for himself and his family, but I also refuse to make that an issue in this campaign. **paralepsis**

3. A movie reviewer writes, "This film lacks coherence in its plot and the acting is unconvincing. However, it is packed with action for those who are satisfied by colliding automobiles and mangled bodies." The movie's promoter uses the review as follows: "One reviewer writes that this movie is 'packed with action'!" **selection**

4. The First Baptist Church burned to the ground this morning. The causes of the fire are under investigation. Without speculating about the fire's origin, it should be noted that the church recently was insured for $2,000,000, and the congregation is known to have debts of about $1,500,000.
arrangement and paralepsis

5. An advocate of sales techniques that included lying to customers about the availability and prices of products defended the practices by claiming, "This is simply a matter of making a persuasive sales presentation." **underdescription**

6. This new handgun registration proposal, which requires a waiting period of one week for purchasing a handgun, as well as a background check on all potential handgun owners, is badly conceived. It says nothing about whether holidays are to be counted as part of the week a person is required to wait.
majoring on minors

7. Representative Baker's opinion on this matter should not be heeded. After all, he's a far left, tax-and-spend liberal! *ad hominem;* **might also be read as poisoning the well**

8. Certainly I believe in UFOs. With all the efforts to disprove their existence, no one yet has succeeded in showing that these are not visitors from other planets.
arguing from ignorance

9. Programs for the gifted are impractical, because determining a child's giftedness presents a critical problem. How are we to determine where to draw the line between the gifted child and others? If we draw the line at, say, a GPA of 3.85, do we deny gifted programs to children with a GPA of 3.83? Because these determinations are impossible to make, and because the gifted programs depend on making these determinations, gifted programs should be abandoned.
continuum fallacy

10. All Catholics should back this new legislation that pays for private schools through an additional city tax. Why? Because it will ensure that parochial schools maintain their tax-exempt status. **ad populum fallacy**

11. Your opinion on the new sexual harassment policy is irrelevant. After all, what can a man know about these things? **poisoning the well**

12. Concerns have been raised that artificially raising human intelligence by genetic engineering to levels that routinely exceed an IQ of 170 would usher in a new species—the post-human. However, there is no clear means of determining when such a new human has arrived, so I think these fears are unfounded. **continuum fallacy**

13. Senator, will you continue to support United States's essentially unjust anti-Israel policy in the Middle East? **question begging**

B. Identify the appeal being employed in each of the following:

1. You say I should never take the advice of others. But that's ridiculous. If I accept what you are saying, I am taking your advice. ***reductio ad absurdum***

2. Illegal immigration must be stopped, and stopped now! It poses a threat to our health care system, our schools, our economy, and our workforce. Unchecked immigration at our southern border could be the final, mortal blow to the United States as we know it! **emotional appeal**

3. Despite recent interest in our organization on the part of both the media and law enforcement agencies, all loyal members of the Omega Planetary Mission are required to refrain from any contact with the press. This pronouncement comes directly from President and Prophet Valentine M. Smith. **appeal to authority**

C. The straw man fallacy is common in public debate when an opponent is allowed to summarize an advocate's case. Provide an example from your own experience of the straw man fallacy.

QUIZ

Which fallacy is represented by each of the following?

1. An attorney advocating deceptive courtroom practices defends his courtroom antics by saying, "This is simply a matter of making a vigorous defense of my client." **underdescription**

2. It is impossible to determine when a fetus becomes a human being. Is conception the crucial point? Is it the moment of cellular division, or the point when brain activity begins? Is a fetus human at the time of quickening, or viability? Though we may agree that a newborn is fully human, no such agreement can be reached concerning when the unborn fetus achieves this distinction. Thus, foes of abortion should not force the rest of us to try to make this distinction by pushing legislation that would ban abortions beyond some arbitrary point in a pregnancy. **continuum fallacy**

3. What can you possibly know about this, Bill? You have never lost a loved one. **poisoning the well**

4. Representative Baker's opinion on this matter should not be heeded. After all, he's a communist and a liar! ***ad hominem***

5. Certainly I believe in ghosts. No one has ever convincingly demonstrated that the dead cannot appear to us and communicate with us. **arguing from ignorance**

6. As a member of a labor union, you will want to vote for this bill. It gives unions special exemption from federal disclosure laws. **ad populum fallacy**

7. Who are you to tell me to study harder? You had to leave Harvard for failing to keep an adequate grade point average. **tu quoque fallacy**

TEST ITEMS

True or False

1. T **F** The text dismisses emotional appeals as always unreasonable.
2. **T** F It is important to balance emotional appeals with other types of argumentative forms and other types of evidence.
3. T **F** Even though some speakers and writers are highly skilled at arousing emotions, they do not risk preventing their audiences from critical thinking in making a decision.
4. **T** F Perhaps the best defense of emotional appeals as part of an argumentative case is their ability to place an audience in the appropriate frame of mind for making a decision and acting on it.
5. T **F** The straw man fallacy occurs when we attack an opponent's character.
6. T **F** The appeal to authority usually rests strictly on respect for authority, and does not involve any stated or implied sanction if the authority is not heeded.
7. **T** F A compelling reason for rejecting authority is one that outweighs the authority's claim to legitimate power, and leaves us willing to endure the consequences of such rejection.
8. T **F** The strategy of paralepsis involves trying to get an audience to laugh at an idea by showing it to be ridiculous.
9. T **F** To follow the rule of charity obliges one to provide assistance to one's opponents in a debate.
10. **T** F Underdescription is the fallacy of creating a false sense or meaning by failing to fully describe a proposal or a crucial component in an opponent's case.
11. T **F** The fallacy of appealing to the audience and its interest rather than to the merits of the argument is called the *tu quoque* fallacy.
12. **T** F To dismiss an individual as unqualified to speak on a topic based on some accident of circumstance is called poisoning the well.
13. T **F** Question begging means to raise an important question.
14. T **F** To repeatedly make the same mistake in reasoning is called the continuum fallacy.

Multiple Choice

1. The appeal that asks an audience to recognize an idea as either self-contradictory or as so unreasonable as to be absurd.
    a. underdescription
    <u>b.</u> *reductio ad absurdum*
    c. paralepsis
    d. selection
    e. arrangement fallacy

2. Making a claim about something by stating that you will not bring the topic up or that it is not important.
    a. underdescription
    b. *reductio ad absurdum*
    <u>c.</u> paralepsis
    d. selection
    e. arrangement fallacy

3. Presenting only some of the available evidence so as to achieve a particular impression, while intentionally excluding other evidence that would contradict the suggested interpretation.
    a. underdescription
    b. *reductio ad absurdum*
    c. paralepsis
    <u>d.</u> selection fallacy
    e. arrangement fallacy

4. Creating a false impression by ordering, associating, or grouping items of evidence in a misleading way.
    a. underdescription
    b. *reductio ad absurdum*
    c. paralepsis
    d. selection fallacy
    <u>e.</u> arrangement fallacy

5. Creating a false sense of meaning by failing to fully describe a proposal or a crucial component in an opponent's case.
    <u>a.</u> underdescription
    b. question begging
    c. *ad hominem*
    d. poisoning the well
    e. majoring on minors

6. Assuming that a debatable question has already been answered or addressed.
    a. underdescription
    <u>b.</u> question begging
    c. *ad hominem*
    d. poisoning the well
    e. majoring on minors

7. An argument directed to the audience and its interests rather than to the merits of a case.
	a. underdescription
	b. question begging
	<u>c.</u> *ad populum* fallacy
	d. poisoning the well
	e. majoring on minors

8. Dismissing an individual as unqualified to speak on a topic on the basis of some accident of circumstances.
	a. underdescription
	b. question begging
	c. *ad hominem*
	<u>d.</u> poisoning the well
	e. majoring on minors

9. Focusing attention on minor or inconsequential points to draw attention away from important ones.
	a. underdescription
	b. question begging
	c. *ad hominem*
	d. poisoning the well
	<u>e.</u> majoring on minors

10. Responding to a weakened version of an opponent's case.
	a. linguistic conventions
	b. fallacy of exaggeration
	c. poisoning the well
	<u>d.</u> attacking a straw man
	e. appeal to authority

11. An appeal urging compliance with the directive of some person, group, or document possessing power.
	a. linguistic conventions
	b. fallacy of exaggeration
	c. motivating the argument
	d. attacking a straw man
	<u>e.</u> appeal to authority

12. Arguing that because some idea has not been disproved, it has thus been proved.
	a. underdescription
	b. question begging
	<u>c.</u> arguing from ignorance
	d. poisoning the well
	e. majoring on minors

Terminology

Provide the correct term for the following definitions.

1. The appeal that asks an audience to recognize an idea as either self-contradictory or as so unreasonable as to be absurd. **reductio ad absurdum**

2. Making a claim about something by stating that you will not bring the topic up or that it is not important. **paralepsis**

3. Presenting only some of the available evidence so as to achieve a particular impression. **selection**

4. Creating an impression by the ordering or placement of items in an argument. **arrangement**

5. Creating a false sense of meaning by failing to fully describe a proposal or a crucial component in a case. **underdescription**

6. Assuming that a debatable question has already been answered or addressed. **question begging**

7. An argument directed to the audience and its interests rather than to the merits of a case. **ad populum fallacy**

8. Dismissing an individual as unqualified to speak on a topic based on some accident of circumstances. **poisoning the well**

9. An argument that is formally invalid or so seriously flawed in some other way as to render it unreliable. **fallacy**

10. Focusing attention on minor or inconsequential points in order to draw attention away from important ones. **majoring on minors**

11. Responding to a weakened version of an opponent's case. **attacking a straw man**

12. An appeal urging compliance with the directive of a person, group, or document possessing power. **appeal to authority**

13. Arguing that because an idea has not been disproved, it has thus been proved. **arguing from ignorance**

14. Falsely reasoning that someone who is guilty of an offense has no right to instruct others not to do something similar. **tu quoque fallacy**

15. The obligation to restate an opponent's argument so as to give it a strong interpretation. **rule of charity**

Short Answer

1. Identify two fears common to most people from which fear appeals are derived.

   1. death or physical harm, either to ourselves or to loved ones

   2. loss of health, wealth, or security, as in loss of occupation

   3. deprivation of rights or freedoms

2. Provide three tests of emotional appeals.

   1. Does the emotional appeal appear in the absence of other arguments and evidence?

   2. Is the appeal so powerful that the audience will have difficulty exercising reason?

   3. Does the appeal place the audience in the proper frame of mind for making a reasonable decision?

3. Identify and briefly explain two approaches for achieving a *reductio ad absurdum*.

   1. assuming the argument is true and showing that it leads to an absurd conclusion

   2. setting up a parallel argument that is clearly unreasonable

4. What are the two kinds of reasons that might lead one to reject an appeal to authority?

   1. Is there sufficient reason to heed this authority in this case?

   2. Is this group or individual an authority for me in this case?

5. Identify three fallacies of faulty assumption.

   argument from ignorance, continuum fallacy, question begging

6. Identify three fallacies directed to the person.

   ad hominem, poisoning the well, tu quoque, ad populum

7. Identify three fallacies of case presentation.

   straw man fallacy, majoring on minors, underdescription

8. Identify three fallacies of suggestion.

   paralepsis, selection, arrangement

Application

Identify the following fallacies or appeals.

1. Benson's proposal shouldn't be listened to, because he's a communist, a liar, and just generally a jerk! **ad hominem**

2. All we need do in deciding which side to back in the surrogacy controversy is to think of the children involved. What does it do to a child to be shuttled back and forth from one family to another, called by different names in each, and never assured that either family is really her family? **emotional appeal**

3. The Pope has condemned the use of contraceptives. It is clear that as Catholics we cannot approve their use. **appeal to authority**

4. Ohm's law expresses the relationship between current, voltage, and resistance in electrical circuits. As scientist Paul Davies has suggested, the idea that this law has existed in some timeless, ethereal realm forever, just waiting for someone to build an electrical circuit, is preposterous. This example proves that physical laws do not exist independent of physical events. **reductio ad absurdum is attributed to Davies.**

5. I am not saying that Mr. Smith is a member of the Mafia, but how do you explain the fact that his name regularly shows up in the indexes of books on the mob? **paralepsis**

6. It may be wrong, but the captain said to do it. **appeal to authority**

APPENDICES
Developing and Adapting Your Case

Appendix A
Policy Case Construction: The Structure of Debate

ADDITIONAL EXERCISES

A. Locate a policy argument being advanced in an editorial in a news magazine, newspaper, or online editorial source. Write a two- to three-page analysis of the case, using the criteria set out in this appendix. Identify the specific problem set out in the example you have selected. Address the following questions:

  1. Does the problem section address the stock issues of inherency and significance?
  2. Is the plan clearly presented? Does it appear to show solvency?
  3. Have benefits of the plan been addressed and counter-arguments answered?
  4. Overall, how would you rate the quality of the editorial as a policy case?

  [If this is used as a written assignment to be presented in class, it is important that the other students have had an opportunity to read the original editorial.]

B. Identify an important, controversial social problem that interests you. Put yourself in the place of the editorial writer and compose a 700-word policy case in response to the problem. Use the criteria set out in this appendix to guide the development of your case.

  [This exercise makes a good written assignment that can be presented in class. Other members of the class can be assigned the task of asking questions.]

C. Identify the specific problem set out in the argument on the food industry in this appendix. Does the problem section satisfy the criteria presented in the appendix? Is the plan clearly presented? Does it appear to address the problem? What kinds of arguments can you identify in the speech? Is each well developed? Overall, how would you rate the quality of this case?

D. Find a policy argument in a major magazine or newspaper. Analyze the case according to the criteria set out in this appendix. Identify and assess arguments in the essay.

E. Do an analysis of a policy argument you have yourself developed for another class or because of your involvement in an interest group. Suggest changes you might make in the argument.

TEST ITEMS

True or False

1. T _F_ *Prima facie* means a conclusive or irrefutable case against an idea or course of action.
2. _T_ F "Inherency" refers to the affirmative case's obligation to show that a problem results directly from the current way of doing things.

3. <u>T</u> F   The status quo has presumption until a *prima facie* case has been advanced against it.
4. T <u>F</u>   Establishing a need and showing a plan's practicality are the only two obligations of the affirmative case in a policy debate.
5. T <u>F</u>   Satisfying the burden of proof means that the affirmative case has been proved beyond any reasonable doubt.
6. <u>T</u> F   A good policy case has an informative as well as a persuasive function.
7. T <u>F</u>   In a policy debate, the negative side has the obligation of establishing harms.
8. <u>T</u> F   Solvency is the stock issue which establishes that the plan advanced represents an effective and practical solution to the problem.
9. T <u>F</u>   When arguing the benefits of a plan, it is all right to speculate about improbable benefits.
10. <u>T</u> F   The benefits of a plan should appear to be significant.
11. T <u>F</u>   The stock issue of topicality is concerned with demonstrating the seriousness of the problem.
12. T <u>F</u>   Structural inherency refers to current attitudes or beliefs that contribute to harms.
13. <u>T</u> F   Showing the imminence of a problem means proving that serious problems are already, or soon will be, produced by the status quo.

Multiple Choice

1. The policy presently in place.
    a.   presumption
    <u>b.</u>   status quo
    c.   *prima facie* case
    d.   case
    e.   negative case

2. Arguments sufficient to raise a significant question regarding the status quo.
    a.   presumption
    b.   status quo
    <u>c.</u>   *prima facie* case
    d.   case
    e.   negative case

3. A test of a policy case that asks whether problems result directly from the status quo and are not caused by extraneous or accidental circumstances.
    <u>a.</u>   inherency
    b.   workability
    c.   practicality
    d.   presumption
    e.   adequacy

Appendix A   Policy Case Construction: The Structure of Debate   161

4. This term describes the affirmative case's obligation to show that the plan would represent an effective and practical solution to a problem.
   a. inherency
   b. workability
   c. practicality
   d. presumption
   <u>e.</u> solvency

5. The affirmative case's obligation to provide sufficient evidence in support of an assertion.
   a. presumption
   b. status quo
   <u>c.</u> burden of proof
   d. affirmative case
   e. negative case

6. A case supporting the status quo.
   a. presumption
   b. adequate case
   c. burden of proof
   d. affirmative case
   <u>e.</u> negative case

7. The requirement to demonstrate that the status quo already has, or soon will have, serious and undesirable consequences.
   <u>a.</u> imminence
   b. novelty
   c. practicality
   d. solvency
   e. ethicality

8. A case challenging the status quo.
   a. presumption
   <u>b.</u> affirmative case
   c. *prima facie* case
   d. evidence case
   e. negative case

9. When a plan is workable and overcomes obstacles, it has been shown to have this quality.
   a. imminence
   b. novelty
   <u>c.</u> practicality
   d. severity
   e. ethicality

10. Criteria governing the soundness of an affirmative case.
    a. presumption
    <u>b.</u> stock issues
    c. *prima facie* case
    d. inherency
    e. harms

11. Stock issues in a debate include
    a. inherency
    b. significance
    c. solvency
    d. topicality
    <u>e.</u> all of the above

Terminology

1. When a policy is accepted as true or adequate without requiring proof, it is said to enjoy this status. **presumption**

2. A case that, prior to being challenged, appears to provide sound evidence for an assertion. ***prima facie* case**

3. The test of a policy case that asks whether the plan represents an effective and practical solution to a problem. **solvency**

4. A plan that has the potential for addressing the problem expediently and is capable of overcoming financial and other obstacles to its implementation has this quality. **practicality**

5. The obligation to provide sufficient evidence in support of an assertion. **burden of proof**

6. The requirement to show that the status quo already has or will soon have serious, undesirable consequences. **imminence**

7. A case supporting the status quo. **negative case**

8. A case challenging the status quo. **affirmative case**

9. Unanticipated benefits that would result from implementing the proposed plan. **novel benefits**

10. Benefits likely to attend a proposed plan. **probable benefits**

11. Criteria governing the soundness of an affirmative case. **stock issues**

12. A stock issue that asks whether the problems or harms are inherent, resulting directly from the status quo. **inherency**

13. A stock issue intended to keep the debate focused on issues relevant to the topic at hand. **topicality**

Appendix B
Adapting Arguments to an Audience

ADDITIONAL EXERCISES

A. For each of the following controversial statements, suggest three beliefs, values, or assumptions that a person who accepts the statement might hold.

[Have students discuss the beliefs, values, and assumptions they have come up with.]

1. The minimum wage should be increased.
2. A first-time conviction for drunk driving should carry a mandatory jail sentence.
3. Adoption records should be made available readily to adoptees.
4. Genetic engineering research should be stopped immediately.
5. Development of nuclear power should be pursued aggressively.
6. Animal experimentation should be halted.
7. Violence in sports should be prosecuted under local criminal statutes.
8. Retirement at age sixty-five should be mandatory for all jobs.
9. Insurance companies should be allowed to ask applicants whether they have AIDS.
10. Registration should be required for all guns.

B. Write an argument, about a page in length, defending any one of the controversial statements listed in exercise A. Write the argument with your class in mind. Use the suggestions in this appendix to adapt your argument to your audience. In the margins of your paper, note the places where you followed certain suggestions.

C. Identify demographic and likely attitudinal elements for the following audience. Suggest ways the speaker might adapt a message to this audience.

A group of deer hunters gathered at a public hall in a **midwestern** state to hear a presentation on new regulations that affected their sport. The three hundred audience members were all **male** and **US citizens of European descent.** Most of the audience members were **wage-earning blue-collar workers** rather than professionals such as doctors and attorneys. The majority were between the ages of **thirty-five and sixty.**

They are uniformly **opposed to the new regulations** that limit hunting areas and increase hunting fees. They are also **not favorably disposed toward the speaker** they were about to hear or to his message—a state Department of Natural Resources representative assigned to address this group on the benefits of the new regulations. **The speaker does not know any members of his audience personally.**

This speaker—facing a hostile audience—might try candor. In addition, the speaker might try to make a connection with a value the audience holds, such as maintaining the number and good health of the animals they hunt. Hunters typically support efforts to maintain animal habitats and are often knowledgeable about problems associated with too many or too few animals in an area.

D. What advice might you offer this advocate based on the following analysis of her audiences?

At a public rally to draw media attention to her campaign, a political candidate running for the United States Senate faces a demographically mixed and largely friendly audience—women and men of various ages, races, and income levels. Her audience's attitudes are already largely aligned with her own, and she will face no unfriendly questions following her speech. The audience is generally friendly to her and to her views.

A little later the same week, however, she is to meet her opponent for the Senate seat in a televised debate before a small audience of reporters and invited guests. This small audience is demographically less diverse than the previous audience. All twenty-three audience members are highly educated, professional people, most of them between thirty and fifty years of age. Most are white males, though a few are women or members of minority groups. The journalists are trained to ask probing questions and to assess evidence. Several are known to be hostile to the candidate's views. A question and answer session follows the debate.

The speaker should seek to reinforce values held in common with the first audience by providing them with any new evidence she is aware of that supports her own and her audience's views.

This friendly audience should not lull her into complacency about facing a hostile audience. She needs to have evidence for her views readily at hand.

She also needs to be able to emphasize values that she shares with the second audience.

[Students will suggest other possibilities based on recommendations made in the chapter.]

TEST ITEMS

True or False

1. <u>T</u> F In most cases arguments are advanced to persuade an audience, which usually means adapting the arguments to the audience.
2. <u>T</u> F Successful case presentation requires gaining an accurate sense of the nature of the audience and adapting your arguments to that audience.
3. T <u>F</u> A well-constructed argument will usually convince an audience even if it is not adapted to that audience.
4. T <u>F</u> Though a speaker should consider an audience's attitude toward his or her topic, it is not important to consider the audience's attitude toward the speaker.
5. <u>T</u> F Some questions about an audience simply do not yield to demographic analysis.
6. <u>T</u> F Candor, or admitting that you recognize a difference of opinion exists, can be helpful when facing a hostile audience.
7. <u>T</u> F When an audience knows it must make a choice, you may devote less time to developing their interest in the topic and more time to urging them to a particular action.
8. T <u>F</u> A well-constructed argument will always be convincing, whether or not the actual audience has been considered.
9. <u>T</u> F Values analysis considers such factors as the audience's religious affiliations and political principles.
10. <u>T</u> F Dispositional analysis is aimed at discovering an audience's attitudes toward your topic and toward you as an advocate.

Multiple Choice

1. When addressing a hostile audience it can be helpful to
    a. admit that you recognize a difference of opinion exists.
    b. indicate that you will not back down.
    c. connect your topic to the audience's values or interests.
    d. show that you take audience concerns seriously.
    <u>e.</u> a, c, and d

2. Values analysis takes into consideration
    a. religious affiliation
    b. beliefs
    c. political principles
    d. political affiliations
    <u>e.</u> all of the above

3. What type of audience analysis considers such factors as age, economic status, and race?
    <u>a.</u> demographic analysis
    b. situation analysis
    c. attitude analysis
    d. values analysis
    e. dispositional analysis

4. What type of audience analysis considers factors such as level of interest and attitudes toward the topic?
    a. demographic analysis
    b. situation analysis
    c. attitude analysis
    d. values analysis
    <u>e.</u> dispositional analysis

Terminology

1. The type of audience analysis that presents a picture of the audience that focuses on descriptive information such as age, race, gender, and economic status. **demographic analysis**

2. Deeply held individual moral convictions acquired from family, cultural background, religious training, and personal experience. **values**

3. The effort to ascertain an audience's beliefs, values, and other moral commitments. **values analysis**

4. The type of audience analysis that considers such factors as attitudes toward the topic, level of interest, and need for information. **dispositional analysis**

5. Seeking an accurate sense of the nature of your audience. **audience analysis**

Short Answer

1. List three questions that can be asked to help get at an audience's beliefs and attitudes.
    1. What audience beliefs are relevant to my argument?
    2. What values do audience members hold that bear on my position?
    3. What is their political perspective?
    4. How strongly do they feel about the issues I am raising?

2. List three questions that might help in a demographic analysis of an audience.
    1. How old are the audience members?
    2. What is their income level?
    3. Where do they live?
    4. What percentage of the audience is female or male?
    5. What racial or ethnic groups are represented in the audience?
    6. What professions are represented?

3. What three types of audience analysis does the text recommend as you construct a picture of the audience?

    demographic profile, values analysis, dispositional analysis

4. List three questions suggested by dispositional analysis that can help with audience analysis.
    1. Is this audience likely to be friendly or hostile toward my position on the topic?
    2. Is this audience likely to be interested in my topic?
    3. Does the audience need information on this topic?
    4. Must members of this audience make a decision about my topic?
    5. What is the audience's attitude toward me?

5. Identify any two of the three suggestions the text makes for adapting your case to a hostile audience.
    1. Use candor: admit that you recognize a difference of opinion exists between you and your audience.
    2. Tell your audience that you take their concerns seriously.
    3. Connect your topic to the audience's values or interests.

Exams and Written Assignments

Exam I
Chapters 1–10

1. Scan and diagram the following argument.

    Most people in the United States take for granted that high quality health care will always be available, but consider that enrollments at medical schools have declined steadily for the past five years. Moreover, in some states, obstetricians are refusing to deliver babies, because the number of obstetric malpractice suits has skyrocketed over the past fifteen years. In addition, more than 25 percent of currently practicing nurses are actively seeking careers outside of medicine! This is because the AIDS epidemic continues to expose nurses to a significant health threat. Such severe health threats are the leading cause of nurses leaving the profession. All this evidence suggests that the United States will soon face a severe shortage of health care providers, so we must act now to protect all medical professionals from the forces driving them from the practice of medicine.

2. Cheryl is not a member of the union unless she is employed at the main plant. She must be employed at the main plant, because she is a member of the union.

    a. Put this conditional argument into a standard if-then form. Rewrite the entire argument, not just the conditional statement.

    b. State what occurs in the argument's second reason.

    c. Is the argument valid or invalid? Watch the indicators carefully.

3. What are the three general criteria of any reasonable argument? Provide the names and one-sentence definitions.

4. The following argument has already been scanned. Standardize the argument:

    A: The government should invest all Social Security funds in the stock market, because B: this would generate enough money to keep Social Security viable and because C: investing such huge amounts in the stock market would stimulate the economy.

5. Provide the terms for the following definitions:

    a. A thoroughly successful rebuttal, one that clearly demonstrates a flaw in the original argument.

    b. Two reasons that must work together to lend support to their conclusion.

    c. A belief, value, assumption, or generalization that links a piece of evidence to a conclusion.

    d. A word or phrase that signals a reason or a conclusion in an argument.

    e. The kind of argument that typically moves from a general principle to a specific application of that principle to a particular case.

6. Identify and briefly define any three virtues of an ethical advocate, as discussed in the text.

7. Identify the following argument by name:

   Ames would only have committed treason for money or romantic reasons, or because of political commitments. He has no political commitments to speak of and he has been quite faithful to his wife. So he must have been seeking money.

8. Provide the rule of validity for enumerative arguments and apply this rule to the following argument. Is the argument valid?

   Either we support a large and unpopular tax increase, or we pass along a huge financial problem to future generations. It is not right to burden future generations with the results of our financial mismanagement. Thus, I say, it is time to raise taxes!

9. For the following generalization, identify the (a) sample, (b) population, (c) property, (d) finding, (e) extent, and (f) absolute sample size.

   A majority of the city's 6 million residents oppose the mayor's plan to privatize city bus services. A recent survey of 1,100 people living within the city limits showed that 67 percent of those surveyed believed the City Transit Authority should manage bus services.

10. Identify the three types of testimony advanced in each of the following examples:

    a. You and your best friend testify that a famous golfer promised to give the two of you his first place winnings from the U.S. Open to finance an extended and much-needed trip to Europe.

    b. The commuter flight's pilot testified that his failure to radio his position to the tower caused yesterday's accident, in which three people died.

11. Two of the three tests of the representativeness of a sample are size and randomness. Identify by name and briefly define the third test.

12. Identify and briefly define any three of the general tests of evidence discussed in the text.

13. In addition to traditional forms such as conversation, public speaking, nonfiction prose, and talk shows, identify two other forms that the text identifies as means of expressing arguments.

14. Stephen Toulmin's term for a generalization that links data to claim.

15. Identify three benefits of the two-sidedness of controversial argument.

Exam I: Answers

1. Scan and diagram the following argument.

   A: Most people in the United States take for granted that high quality health care will always be available, <u>but consider that</u> B: enrollments at medical schools have declined steadily for the past five years. <u>Moreover</u>, C: in some states, obstetricians are refusing to deliver babies, <u>because</u> D: the number of obstetric malpractice suits has skyrocketed over the past fifteen years. <u>In addition</u>, E: more than 25 percent of currently practicing nurses are actively seeking careers outside of medicine! <u>This is because</u> F: the AIDS epidemic continues to expose nurses to a significant health threat. [and] G: Such severe health threats are the leading cause of nurses leaving the profession. <u>All this evidence suggests that</u> H: the United States will soon face a severe shortage of health care providers, <u>so</u> I: we must act now to protect all medical professionals from the forces driving them from the practice of medicine.

   ## Diagram

   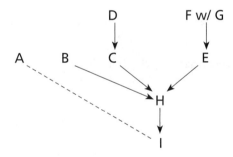

2. Cheryl is not a member of the union unless she is employed at the main plant. She must be employed at the main plant, because she is a member of the union.

   a. Put this conditional argument into a standard if-then form. Rewrite the entire argument, not just the conditional statement.

   If she is not employed at the main plant, then Cheryl is not a member of the union.

   She is a member of the union.

   So

   She must be employed at the main plant.

   b. State what occurs in the argument's second reason.

   Denies the consequent.

   c. Is the argument valid or invalid? Watch the indicators carefully.

   It is valid.

3. What are the three general criteria of any reasonable argument? Provide the names and one-sentence definitions.

   Support: The strength and accuracy of the evidence.

   Validity: A solid internal structure that allows for reasonable connections between evidence and conclusions.

   Linguistic consistency: Clarity and consistency of language; the use of terms in the same way throughout the argument.

4. The following argument has already been scanned. Standardize the argument:

   because

   B: [Investing all Social Security funds in the stock market] would generate enough money to keep Social Security viable

   and because

   C: Investing such huge amounts in the stock market would stimulate the economy.

   [Thus]

   A: The government should invest all Social Security funds in the stock market.

5. Provide the terms for the following definitions.

   a. A thoroughly successful rebuttal, one that clearly demonstrates a flaw in the original argument. **refutation**

   b. Two reasons that must work together to lend support to their conclusion. **complementary reasons**

   c. A belief, value, assumption, or generalization that links a piece of evidence to a conclusion. **connective**

   d. A word or phrase that signals a reason or a conclusion in an argument. **indicator**

   e. The kind of argument that typically moves from a general principle to a specific application of that principle to a particular case. **deductive argument**

6. Identify and briefly define any three virtues of an ethical advocate, as discussed in the text.

Honesty: Fidelity to what is the case, a tendency not to willingly mislead, a regard for what is or what we take to be true.

Courage in argument: A willingness to accept the risk associated with open advocacy of one's position, even when that position is unpopular or dangerous.

Respect for persons: A regard for others as reasoning persons.

Cooperation: A willingness to engage the argumentative process so that a just resolution of the issues can be achieved.

Regard for contexts: A willingness to create and preserve settings for argumentation to occur, cultivate the relationships in which it occurs, and allow the argumentative process to continue as long as necessary to ensure reasonable resolution of issues.

7. Identify the following argument by name:

Ames would only have committed treason for money or romantic reasons, or because of political commitments. He has no political commitments to speak of and he has been quite faithful to his wife. So he must have been seeking money.
enumeration argument

8. Provide the rule of validity for enumerative arguments and apply this rule to the following argument. Is the argument valid?

Either we support a large and unpopular tax increase, or we pass along a huge financial problem to future generations. It is not right to burden future generations with the results of our financial mismanagement. Thus, I say, it is time to raise taxes!

1. Set out the alternative options, then follow a process of elimination.

2. The argument is valid. One option is eliminated—passing along a huge financial problem to future generations.

9. For the following generalization, identify the (a) sample, (b) population, (c) property, (d) finding, (e) extent, and (f) absolute sample size.

A majority of the city's 6 million residents oppose the mayor's plan to privatize city bus services. A recent survey of 1,100 people living within the city limits showed that 67 percent of those surveyed believed the City Transit Authority should manage bus services.

a. Sample: 1,100 people living within the city limits

b. Population: the city's 6 million residents

c: Property: oppose the mayor's plan to privatize city bus services.

d. Finding: 67 percent of those surveyed believed the City Transit Authority should manage bus services.

e. Extent: a majority

f: Absolute sample size: 1,100

10. Identify the three types of testimony advanced in each of the following examples:

   a. You and your best friend testify that a famous golfer promised to give the two of you his first place winnings from the U.S. Open to finance an extended and much-needed trip to Europe.

   concurrent, lay, biased testimony

   b. The commuter flight's pilot testified that his failure to radio his position to the tower caused yesterday's accident in which three people died.

   individual, reluctant, expert testimony

11. Two of the three tests of the representativeness of a sample are size and randomness. Identify by name and briefly define the third test.

   Stratification: This test asks whether the sample adequately reflects the groups and variations within the population.

12. Identify and briefly define any three of the general tests of evidence discussed in Chapter 6.

   Accessibility: The evidence is available for examination.

   Internal consistency: The evidence should not contradict itself.

   External consistency: The evidence should not be sharply at odds with either the majority of evidence from other sources or with the best evidence from other sources.

   Recency: The evidence should be up-to-date and not superseded by more timely evidence.

   Relevance: The evidence should have bearing on the conclusion.

   Adequacy: The evidence, when taken together, should be sufficient to support its claim.

13. In addition to traditional forms such as conversation, public speaking, nonfiction prose, and talk shows, identify two other forms that the text identifies as means of expressing arguments.

   songs, novels, movies, photographs, photojournalism, visual images

14. Stephen Toulmin's term for a generalization that links data to claim.

   warrant

15. Identify three benefits of the two-sidedness of controversial argument.

   1. **Disagreements are aired.**
   2. **Ideas are tested.**
   3. **Positions are refined.**

Exam II
Chapters 11–18, Appendices A and B

1. Provide the three rules of validity for categorical arguments.

2. Write out the following argument in standard form. Identify the statements by type (e.g., particular affirmative, etc.). Mark the distribution of all terms using **D** and **U** in all three statements. Identify the middle term (**MT**) and end terms (**ET**). Test for validity and indicate whether any rules have been broken.

    Some migratory birds are not omnivorous because some migratory birds are not songbirds, and all omnivorous birds are songbirds.

3. Provide the three tests of a hypothesis argument in the form of three questions.

4. Identify (a) the observation that needs an explanation and (b) two alternative hypotheses in the following news item:

    Many people who have suffered the tragic loss of a beloved dog or cat report that the animal has visited them again, either in a dream or in real life. Dr. Lynn Friday doesn't laugh when people tell her their deceased pets have contacted them. The Lexington, Kentucky, veterinarian believes the spirits of some pets stick around their owners for weeks, even months, before disappearing. "Our pets love us, and don't want to leave us," she said. Other vets disagree with Friday. Dr. William Burrows said he does not believe in a "lingering spirit," but does believe there is a "space in people's minds where there is emptiness and grieving" and that causes the sense that the pet is still present.

5. Identify the evidence case, conclusion case, and conclusion of the following analogy. What type of analogy is it?

    The United States provided military assistance to help Kuwait. Thus, it is only fair that we provide similar help to the embattled refugees in the Darfur region of Sudan.

6. In reasoning to a causal generalization from correlation alone, two problems may arise. The first is the possibility of mistaking the cause for the effect, that is, pointing the causal arrow in the wrong direction. What is the other potential problem associated with reasoning to cause from correlation alone? It is reflected in the following advertisement:

    A recent study of corporate executives demonstrates that the most successful also have the largest vocabularies. Thus, increasing your vocabulary will lead to business success.

7. List two tests of a literal analogy.

8. Identify the evidence relationship and the conclusion relationship in the following figurative analogy.

> Ordinary investors buying foreign stocks from anonymous agents over the Internet are engaged in a dangerous game of speculation with potentially disastrous consequences. Even though the investors may succeed by dumb luck, they simply don't know what they are doing, and could lose everything. It's a little like going swimming in an area where sharks have been reported. You might be OK, but you might get eaten alive.

9. Identify the fallacies defined below:

   a. A fallacy that claims that because something has not been disproved, it has thus been proved.

   b. A fallacy that creates a false impression by ordering, associating, or grouping items of evidence in a misleading way.

   c. A fallacy that involves making a claim by stating that you will not bring a matter up or that it is insignificant.

10. Define the following terms:
    a. *prima facie* case
    b. negative case
    c. harms
    d. values analysis
    e. dispositional analysis

11. A name for any categorical statement in which the subject and predicate terms are distributed similarly.

12. Two tests of narrative argument that consider factors both internal and external to the story's plot.

13. Provide any example of visual argument discussed in the text.

14. A recent headline read: "Youths fast to help needy." The story indicated that the youths were going without food to raise money to help poor people, not that they were quick to help needy people. Is this a case of ambiguity or of equivocation?

15. What source of definition is reflected in the following example?

> The Supreme Court has defined a "disability" as any condition that prevents the normal performance of any major life function.

Exam II: Answers

1. Provide the three rules of validity for categorical arguments.

   1. The middle term must be distributed exactly once.

   2. Neither end term may be distributed only once.

   3. The number of negative reasons must equal the number of negative conclusions.

2. Write out the argument in standard form. Identify the statements by type (e.g. particular affirmative, etc.) Mark the distribution of all terms using **D** and **U** in all three statements. Identify the Middle Term (**MT**) and end terms (**ET**). Check for validity.

            U   D
   Some / migratory birds / are not / songbirds /.

          D   U
   All / omnivorous birds / are / songbirds /.

   Therefore

          U   D
   Some / migratory birds / are not / omnivorous /.

   MT: Songbirds

   ET: Migrating birds

        Omnivorous birds

   The argument is valid.

   No rules have been broken.

3. Provide the three tests of a hypothesis argument in the form of three questions.

   1. Does the hypothesis account adequately for the event?

   2. Has a similar hypothesis been shown to be accurate in analogous cases?

   3. Is there an alternative hypothesis that better explains the observation?

4. Identify (a) the observation that needs an explanation and (b) two alternative hypotheses in the following news item:

> Many people who have suffered the tragic loss of a beloved dog or cat report that the animal has visited them again, either in a dream or in real life. Dr. Lynn Friday doesn't laugh when people tell her their dead pets have contacted them. The Lexington, Kentucky, veterinarian believes the spirits of some pets stick around their owners for weeks, even months, before disappearing. "Our pets love us, and don't want to leave us," she said. Other vets disagree with Friday. Dr. William Burrows said he does not believe in a "lingering spirit," but does believe there is a "space in people's minds where there is emptiness and grieving" and that causes the sense that the pet is still present.

Observation: People report that their deceased pets visit them.

Hypothesis 1: People are actually contacted by the spirit of the dead pet that is "hanging around."

Hypothesis 2: There is a "space in people's minds" where there is emptiness and grieving.

5. Identify the evidence case, conclusion case, and conclusion of the following analogy. What type of analogy is it?

> The United States provided military assistance to help Kuwait. Thus, it is only fair that we provide similar help to the embattled refugees in the Darfur region of Sudan.

Evidence case: military assistance to Kuwait

Conclusion case: military assistance to Darfur region of Sudan

Conclusion: Thus, it is only fair that we provide similar help to the embattled refugees of Sudan.

Type of analogy: judicial

6. In reasoning to a causal generalization from correlation alone, two problems may arise. The first is the possibility of mistaking the cause for the effect, that is, pointing the causal arrow in the wrong direction. What is the other potential problem associated with reasoning to cause from correlation alone? It is reflected in the following advertisement:

> A recent study of corporate executives demonstrates that the most successful also have the largest vocabularies. Thus, increasing your vocabulary will lead to business success.

Failure to identify a hidden third factor that is the cause of both events, in this case, education.

7. List two tests of a literal analogy.

Are the two cases being compared dissimilar in some critical respect?

Are the two cases presented accurately?

Is a better analogy available?

8. Identify the evidence relationship and the conclusion relationship in the following figurative analogy.

Ordinary investors buying foreign stocks from anonymous agents over the Internet are engaged in a dangerous game of speculation with potentially disastrous consequences. Even though the investors may succeed by dumb luck, they simply don't know what they are doing, and could lose everything. It's a little like going swimming in an area where sharks have been reported. You might be OK, but you might get eaten alive.

Evidence relationship: swimmers / sharks

Conclusion relationship: investors / anonymous stock agents

9. Identify the fallacies defined below:

a. A fallacy that claims that because something has not been disproved, it has thus been proved. **argument from ignorance**

b. A fallacy that creates a false impression by ordering, associating, or grouping items of evidence in a misleading way. **arrangement fallacy**

c. A fallacy that involves making a claim by stating that you will not bring a matter up or that it is insignificant. **paralepsis**

10. Define the following terms:

a. *prima facie* case **A case that, prior to being challenged, appears to provide sound evidence for an assertion.**

b. negative case **In a policy debate, a series of arguments supporting the status quo.**

c. harms **In policy debate, a problem or problems resulting from the status quo.**

d. values analysis **In audience analysis, the effort to ascertain an audience's beliefs, values, and other moral commitments.**

e. dispositional analysis **Audience analysis aimed at ascertaining audience attitude toward your topic and perhaps toward you as the speaker.**

11. A name for any categorical statement in which the subject and predicate terms are distributed similarly.

convertible statement

12. Two tests of narrative argument that consider factors both internal and external to the story's plot.

coherence and fidelity

13. Provide any example of visual argument discussed in the text.

skyscrapers in Shanghai; photographs (including, but not only, photojournalism or news photos); building design; Martin Luther King Jr., on the steps of the Lincoln Memorial; advertisements

14. A recent headline read: "Youths fast to help needy." The story indicated that the youths were going without food to raise money to help poor people, not that they were quick to help needy people. Is this a case of ambiguity or of equivocation? **ambiguity**

15. What source of definition is reflected in the following example?

    The Supreme Court has defined a "disability" as any condition that prevents the normal performance of any major life function. **authority**

Written Assignments

A. This assignment involves selecting an editorial on any topic and writing a thorough analysis of its arguments. You will need to show the instructor the editorial or other essay you select *before* you begin your analysis work. I want to be sure you have selected the right kind of text, and I do not want to see two analyses of the same essay.

In your analysis, which should run about four pages, be sure to:

1. Identify the essay's conclusion or main contention.

2. Identify by name the different arguments and strategies advanced in support of the essay's conclusion.

3. Explain how the author uses these arguments and strategies to support the main contention. That is, explain how the argumentative case develops.

4. Evaluate the essay's arguments by applying the appropriate tests from the text and assess the strength of the case. You need not render a positive assessment of the essay. You do need to answer the general question: Is this a reasonable case?

You may find potential essays for analysis in the opinion columns of news magazines, editorial pages of newspapers, literature of lobbying groups, letters sent out by advocacy groups, the Internet, or other sources. The only requirements for the editorial you select are that it must:

1. Be between 600 and 800 words in length.

2. Clearly advocate and argue for a position.

3. Be published within the last six months.

The best essays for this assignment are built around a clear, structural argument and advance a variety of other arguments and evidence. *Do not select a news report for this assignment.*

B. For this assignment, you will write a 700-word (3 pages, double-spaced) editorial essay on a topic that is of interest to you and that represents a national controversy. The essay should meet the following criteria:

1. Develops around a **clear thesis** or claim that appears at least once in the essay.

2. Develops a **factual** (usually these are **causal**), **evaluative,** or **policy case** around at least *three different lines of argument* in support of your thesis. These arguments should be labeled in bold print in your paper following the presentation of each argument (e.g., **pragmatic argument**). Be sure to **label all arguments** you use to develop your case.

3. Takes as its starting point some **fact, statistic, quotation,** or other **observation.** Your model is a newspaper or news magazine column of the type you analyzed in the previous assignment. For example, your essay might present facts suggesting a problem for which you advance a solution. Or, you might explore a situation that you think needs a causal explanation, and then provide one.

4. Incorporates as **evidence** at least four statistics, instances of testimony, or other support drawn from at least three different sources, which you both footnote and cite in the text of your essay. One of these sources must have been published within the last four months. Please note: *Any claim you make that is not a matter of common knowledge must be supported by evidence.*

Your goal is to argue persuasively a proposition of fact, value, or policy, and to adapt your argument effectively to your audience. Direct your essay as a response to some fact or observation that you think indicates a serious problem facing US society. For example, you might respond to a fact such as:

The United States incarcerates a higher percentage of its citizens than any other industrialized country.

Or

The largest legal industry in our country is gambling.

Or

The dropout rate in some US cities is higher than 60 percent.

Again, at least three sources should be footnoted and cited in the text of your essay. At least one of these should have been published within the last four months.

The point of this exercise is to argue a single, limited thesis persuasively in three pages. Your essay should be designed to express your opinion to others, to prompt their thought on an important point, and to persuade them to your point of view. Your claim should be clear, your arguments easily understood and convincing, and your writing engaging. You will present your piece to the class during the last two weeks of the semester.

Arguing a proposition of fact: The fact must be significant and represent an interpretation of available evidence that is not likely to achieve general agreement. That is, you need to argue for a particular interpretation of the available evidence. You should present evidence regarding the issue being contested and clearly interpret that evidence so as to support your factual contention. An example of a proposition of fact might be: The cause of the crisis in Kosovo is the United States's weak foreign policy.

Arguing a proposition of value: A proposition of value must be accompanied by criteria of evaluation. These criteria must be set out clearly and direct application made to the object being evaluated. Evidence should be provided to persuade the audience that the evaluation is accurate. An example of a proposition of value might be: The declining image of the United States overseas is a serious threat to our economic stability.

Arguing a proposition of policy: Propositions of policy must be supported by evidence of a problem that is serious and inherent to the way things currently are done (the status quo), as discussed in Appendix A. A policy or plan must be advanced and supported by arguments that show that it is practical and that it will actually solve the problem. An example of a proposition of policy might be: The NCAA should act to ensure that women's athletic programs receive the same funding as men's athletics in all divisions.

Your thesis should reflect a controversy, and the controversy should not be a local one. Issues of concern here are acceptable as topics as long as they are of concern beyond your school.

Please do not argue standard debate topics such as legalization of marijuana, gun control, abortion, and euthanasia. If the arguments on a topic are likely to be well known to your audience, avoid the topic. If you want to ask me about exceptions to this restriction, please feel free. For example, an unusual policy addressing a well-known problem may provide an acceptable topic.